DUKE · UNIVERSITY · PUBLICATIONS

THE
SOCIAL PHILOSOPHY OF
WILLIAM MORRIS

London:
CAMBRIDGE UNIVERSITY PRESS

New York:
G. E. STECHERT & CO.

Tokyo:
MARUZEN AND COMPANY, LTD.

Shanghai:
EDWARD EVANS & SONS, LTD.

WILLIAM MORRIS

THE

SOCIAL PHILOSOPHY

OF

WILLIAM MORRIS

BY

ANNA A. von HELMHOLTZ-PHELAN, Ph.D.

DURHAM · NORTH CAROLINA
DUKE UNIVERSITY PRESS
1927

COPYRIGHT 1927
BY DUKE UNIVERSITY PRESS

THE SEEMAN PRESS
DURHAM, N. C.

Printed in the United States of America

To

THE MEMORY OF THE COURAGEOUS
CHIVALROUS AND GREAT-SOULED

WILLIAM MORRIS

APOSTLE OF THE NOBLE IDEAL OF
JOY IN ONE'S WORK—AN
INDISPENSABLE FACTOR
OF WORTHY LIVING

FOREWORD

The biographical chapters of this book emphasize only those influences and events which made William Morris a social thinker. They are in no sense intended to present a full account of his life. That has been most satisfactorily and interestingly done by Mr. J. W. Mackail.

William Morris, Democrat might have been the title of this work. For Morris was a Democrat in that he came to believe in the socialistic theory of the government of industry and of business by the masses; but he displayed also the essential characteristics of the real aristocrat, since he both felt and acted upon a deep sense of responsibility for the well-being of humanity. That it is the essence of chivalry to interfere is the sarcastic comment of a brilliant representative of a race whose knights and soldiers have disappeared in consequence of race persecution. The friend of chivalry admits the truth of this statement, but with the addition that the knight attends to other people's affairs only to defend or to promote justice. William Morris was of the Order of Chivalry, and in an age of reeking smokestacks and of great degradation in the ranks of the empty-handed laborer. He knew that modern industry with its haste, its greed, and its misguided laissez-faire,— even though laissez-faire was an essential step in economic development,—was not giving the soul of man a fair chance, and he therefore attacked modern industry with all the strength and fervor of a great knight.

Would Morris, if he were living to-day, have modified his attitude toward modern industry? Many changes for the better have come about since his time. Machine industry has added much to the comfort of the masses, for it has now taken over a great deal of the degrading, menial work which Morris thought the only justification of the machine; factory buildings are better; hours are shorter; wages are higher; stock ownership by workers has made a fair start; and in America, panics have ceased, and depressions promise to do likewise. As a toiler, the average worker is still necessarily more or less a cog in a great system; but shorter hours, more cheaply produced goods, and wages sufficient to buy them, make of the average worker a great freeman as a buyer or consumer. Modern industry, in a sense, necessarily enslaves; but it also liberates. It cannot be said, however, that art is more flourishing, or on a higher level, and that the soul of man finds any more free expression in the work that he must do to live than in Morris's time. No doubt the better material conditions of to-day express themselves in higher spiritual and cultural values in the lives of the workers. It is a fair question as to whether Morris would still see hope for a happy life for man through a return to simplified production and through the establishment of a democratic régime in industry. He must have come to see that modern production cannot go back to an earlier form, and that not even democracy carried to the nth degree could accomplish such a miracle.

Plutocratic control is not entirely good; but would democratic control be better? The biggest Man Friday, at the time, of American plutocracy, from his sick bed in an eastern state reached out to Chicago, it has been said, to nominate the successor of President Wilson. It is now said that a great plutocrat in that same eastern state will select our next president. This is not entirely good; but would people who allow such a system be able to select better themselves? Their stupidity is necessary to the rule of plutocracy. As for so-called democracy, its biggest curse in America is that a species of democratic opportunity too often puts serf-souled people in high places. It is not improbable that a better America will come, if it does come, through a better plutocracy,—a plutocracy that will promote greater freedom of opportunity,—and an aristocracy in government and in business that will be guided by high ideals of fairness, of efficiency, and even of art, and yet working out in some way a system through which Morris's noble ideal of work-happiness may be fulfilled.

An associate of the author's divides modern society into three groups: those who see *nothing good* in modern capitalism; those who see *nothing bad*; and those who see *both good and bad*,—who expect progress, less injustice, more soul and more art to be achieved through promoting the good and minimizing the bad in autocratically controlled modern production.

The author gladly acknowledges her debt to the spacious spirit of William Morris, to the philosophers and leaders of all times who have influenced her, to her professors at the Universities of Wisconsin and of Berlin, to the Duke University Press, and to its editor, Dr. Paull F. Baum.

Anna Augusta von Helmholtz-Phelan

University of Minnesota
October 22, 1927

TABLE OF CONTENTS

Part I.

The Making of a Democrat

Part II.

The History of Morris's Socialism

Part III.

The Social Ideals of William Morris

PART I

THE
MAKING OF A DEMOCRAT

CHAPTER I

EARLY LIFE AND COLLEGE DAYS

To democratize art and to ennoble and beautify common daily work was the aim of William Morris in his earnest crusade for the cause of art and for the cause of humanity. Morris desired for every human being a fair share of the nobler joys of living and of being. He declared that it is wrong to shut one's eyes to ugliness and to vulgarity wherever found, or to acquiesce in them as either desirable or necessary.[1] Though he approached the social question from the side of art, he was not merely an aesthete. He saw very clearly that economic conditions lie back of the wretchedness, the vulgarity, the narrowness, and the ugliness that too frequently make up the larger part of the life of the masses. He insisted further that the rich, with all of their power and their dominion over the earth, cannot escape from sharing in some degree the degradation of the worker who produces the wares which all must buy, rich and poor alike. The present age, by denying a fair share of the joys and satisfactions of life to the laborer, diminishes the real joys and satisfactions of life for the rich. The vulgarization of the worker lowers the level of life for all.

But William Morris had a long road to travel before he arrived at a formulation of his social ideals. Just as the circumstances of the poor laborer fashion and form his life of restriction and too often of sordid ugliness, so the circumstances of Morris's life brought him only after many years to a complete realization and understanding of the conditions of life. The March to Damascus was as necessary for him as for the many others upon whom a great light has shined.

William Morris, son of William Morris and Emma Shelton, was born at Elm House, Walthamstow, near Epping Forest, March 24, 1834. His father was an

[1] J. W. Mackail, *The Life of William Morris*, I, 305.—Throughout Part I the facts of Morris's life are drawn, except where otherwise indicated, from Mackail. —The subsequent quotations from Mackail are made with the generous permission of the publishers, Messrs. Longmans, Green and Co.

opulent bill-broker of Welsh descent; his mother was the daughter of a music teacher in Worcester. When William was six years old, his family moved to the other side of Epping Forest, to Woodford Hall, a spacious Georgian mansion located in the midst of fifty acres of park, and having attached to it a farm of a hundred acres. These surroundings fostered in Morris a love of nature and an enjoyment of out-door life. His biographer states that Morris was born with a love for the Middle Ages.[2] Be that as it may, it is certain that the environment in which he was placed in his early youth was such as would tend to develop in any child endowed with an imagination a deep interest in ancient things. Woodford Hall, moreover, retained throughout Morris's childhood many of the customs of the self-sufficient life of an old English manor house.[3] It also observed several of the ancient holidays and festivals of England. For example, the Masque of St. George was always performed on Twelfth Night. One of Morris's playthings was a suit of armor, which, it is said, he sometimes wore to ride in Epping Forest. Probably his enjoyment of the suit of armor was partly derived from his poring over Scott's novels, which, we are told, he was reading at the age of four, and had finished by the age of seven.[4] Other books which made a deep impression on him were Lane's *Arabian Nights* and Gerard's *Herbal*. The *Herbal* is said to have given him ideas for some of the patterns of his wall-papers and back-ground designs for his glass and tapestry.

It was important, too, for Morris's development that his father was intensely interested in the old churches near Woodford Hall, for Morris often had the advantage of going with his father on little trips to examine the brasses and monuments of these ancient buildings. Morris himself testifies that when he was only eight years old his father took him to Canterbury and to the church of Minster in Thanet, on which occasion was

[2]Mackail, I, 10.
[3]Alfred Noyes, *William Morris*, p. 3.
[4]Mackail, I, 5-10. See Noyes, p. 3, where he questions Mackail's statement concerning the reading of Scott at the age of four.

made so lasting an impression on his mind of the beauty and glory of Gothic architecture, that fifty years later, without having once seen the Minster in the meantime, he was able to describe it in some detail from the recollection of that one visit. This would certainly indicate in Morris amazing power of observation and more than a stimulated interest in the old buildings of his country. Indeed, the ancient country houses in his locality, some of them dating to the fifteenth and sixteenth centuries, were as well known to him as the churches his father had taken him to see. The impression of romance which a certain room hung with faded greenery in Queen Elizabeth's Lodge in Epping Forest had made upon him as a boy always came back to him whenever he read the description of the Green Room at Monkbarns in Scott's *Antiquary*. It is more than probable that the atmosphere of his first volume of poetry, *The Defence of Guenevere*, owes not a little to these early impressions of romance, these lingerings among stone images and tombs, these loving and reverent examinations of ancient inscription and storied window.

But Morris's interest in medieval romance and architecture, unusual and certainly intelligent though it was, filled his leisure hours rather than his work time; for like most other youngsters in his neighborhood, Morris attended the preparatory school near his home. After his father's death in 1847 he was sent to Marlborough College, where he remained until Christmas, 1851. Fortunately for Morris's future life, the surroundings of Marlborough College were as beautiful and romantic as the surroundings of Woodford Hall. The loose discipline of the school was also favorable to the development of Morris's individuality. It was an individuality, however, fostered rather by solitary rambles in the neighborhood and by loneliness than by active companionship with his fellows. The ordinary games of his schoolmates apparently attracted him not at all. His long walks were not, as might be guessed, devoted to introspection. On these occasions he examined the pre-Celtic long barrows, the round barrows, the stone circles of Avebury, and the Roman villas at Kennet. Certainly an unusual interest, this, for a young schoolboy, and an unusual occupation, too, his incessant netting. His hands had always to be moving. Curious also was his way of amusing the boys who sometimes accompanied him on his walks. He told them endless stories about knights and fairies, one tale growing out of another. And yet he was no bloodless student. He was a robust, healthy boy with courage to be himself at all times.

Morris's reading during his residence at Marlborough College naturally reflected his predilection. Works on archeology and ecclesiastical architecture absorbed him deeply. His interest in churches was strengthened by the High Church tendency at the College, and by the influence of the Anglo-Catholic movement, then beginning to make itself felt. The older church music, sung by a trained choir instituted during his attendance, made a strong appeal in the same direction to his susceptible, romantic nature.

At seventeen Morris left Marlborough College, which for four years had had the good sense to permit him to follow his bent. After reading for a year with a private tutor he entered in 1853 into residence at Exeter College, Oxford, with the idea of taking orders. Everything in his environment seemed to conspire to make Morris a steadfast lover of the Middle Ages. His childhood home, his reading, his preparatory school, and finally Oxford all worked together to stimulate and to deepen an inborn interest in the past. For at the time that Morris matriculated at Oxford, Oxford was a medieval city. Its streets were the streets of the fifteenth century. Its grey-roofed houses and its ancient towers were like a picture of old days. The hand of progress had not even pointed toward Oxford. Naturally it made upon Morris an ineffaceable impression,—an impression recorded by him in fitting words many years later.[5] In the environment of Oxford the tendencies which had been manifest in him from his earliest youth

[5]Mackail, I, 29; and Morris, *Signs of Change*, pp. 123-4.

could not but be strengthened. His new surroundings impelled him more swiftly and with more momentum along the road which he had travelled when he galloped through Epping Forest clad in his little suit of armor, or when he studied the brasses and monuments of ancient churches and houses near Woodford Hall.

But not alone because the enchantment of the Middle Ages still hung about its ancient spires and still pervaded its stately halls was Oxford to be significant in the life of Morris; for at Oxford Morris met Burne-Jones. Never were two young people more congenial, more alike in their tastes. The environment of Oxford was as full of meaning for Burne-Jones as for Morris. Both were destined for the church,—another bond of union. Inevitably they lost no time in laying the foundation of a lifelong friendship. They studied and read incessantly together in theology, in ecclesiastical history, and in ecclesiastical archeology. Naturally followed the study of mythology, history, poetry, and art. Morris especially plunged into an eager study of medieval romances, chronicles, and architecture, not omitting altogether a few modern writers. The combined impact of all of these influences prepared him for an absorbing interest in art. His study of architecture, and his companionship with Burne-Jones, together with his own deep and constant love of nature and of the beautiful in all of its aspects not only impelled him toward art, but were the sources of his lifelong devotion to art.

Canon Dixon has left some interesting reminiscences of the group of young men which Morris and Burne-Jones soon gathered about them, the group afterward developed into the Brotherhood. The bond of alliance among them was not that they were all destined for Holy Orders; it was their common love of poetry and their indefinite literary and artistic aspirations. "We all had the notion," wrote the Canon, "of doing great things for man; in our own way, however, according to our own will and bent."[6] Morris, according to these

[6]Mackail, I, 42.

reminiscences, was at first regarded simply as a pleasant boy who liked to do a great deal of talking in a "husky shout", and who was fond of outdoor life.   But it was not long before his strong personality became a dominant influence in the group.   He was physically very robust, full of fire and impetuosity, and naturally extremely high-tempered.   His friends tell many anecdotes,—some of them doubtless having gained in the telling,—of his uncontrolled temper, and of his habit of beating vigorously his own head and body when displeased or excited.   Not only, however, did his physical qualities and his personality impress themselves speedily and forcibly on the group, but his intellect soon made itself respected.   He was found to be decisive in his judgments and accurate in his statements; his close observation was evident even in his casual and incidental remarks; and his knowledge of things quite outside of their fields,—as, for example, architecture,—soon won him their respect.   The leader of the group was at first Fulford, but "in reality", wrote Dixon, "neither he nor any one else in the world could lead Morris or Burne-Jones".   Dixon's record of Morris at this time is interesting to the student of his social ideals.

At this time Morris was an aristocrat, and a High Churchman. His manners and tastes and sympathies were all aristocratic.   His countenance was beautiful in features and expression, particularly in the expression of purity.   Occasionally it had a melancholy look. He had a finely-cut mouth, the short upper lip adding greatly to the purity of the expression.   I have a vivid recollection of the splendid beauty of his presence at that time.

It was when the Exeter men, Burne-Jones and he, got at Ruskin, that strong direction was given to a true vocation,—*The Seven Lamps, Modern Painters*, and *The Stones of Venice*.   It was some little time before I and the others could enter into this; but we soon saw the greatness and importance of it.   Morris would often read Ruskin aloud.   He had a mighty singing voice, and chanted rather than read those weltering oceans of eloquence as they have never been given before or since, it is most certain.   The description of the Slave Ship, or Turner's skies, with the burden, "Has Claude given this?" were declaimed by him in a manner that made them seem as if they had been written for no end but that he should hurl them in thunder on the head of the base criminal who had never seen what Turner saw in the sky.[7]

In the Long Vacation of 1854 Morris went to Belgium and to Northern France. The churches of Amiens, Beauvais, and Chartres, which he considered to be the noblest achievements of man, henceforth took their places along with the grey stones and the grey streets of the Oxford of his undergraduate days as one of the passionate admirations of his life. In the *Aims of Art*, written many years later, Morris said:

Less than forty years ago I first saw the city of Rouen, then still in its outward aspect a piece of the Middle Ages; no words can tell you how its mingled beauty, history, and romance took hold on me; I can only say that, looking back on my past life, I find it was the greatest pleasure I ever had; and now it is a pleasure which no one can ever have again; it is lost to the world forever. At that time I was an undergraduate of Oxford. Though not so astounding, so romantic, or at first sight so mediaeval as the Norman city, Oxford in those days still kept a great deal of its earlier loveliness; and the memory of its grey streets as they then were, has been an abiding influence and pleasure in my life, and would be greater still if I could only forget what they are now—a matter of far more importance than the so-called learning of the place could have been to me in any case, but which, as it was, no one tried to teach me, and I did not try to learn.[8]

Under the varying influences of university life, with its study of modern and secular literature, of Carlyle and Ruskin, its contact with other personalities, the secularization, as Mackail calls it, of Morris's mind went on rapidly. In 1855 Morris fell under the spell of Chaucer and Browning. To those who have read through Morris's poetry, it is not necessary to make any statement as to the strength of the effect of Chaucer upon him; and to those who know his first volume of poems, the effect of Browning, especially upon his form, is apparent almost to the same degree. Added to these was

[7]Mackail, I, 43 ff. See also Morris, *Architecture, Industry and Wealth*, pp.204-05. Of Ruskin Morris always spoke in later years as his master, giving him the credit of awakening him to the social aspects of art; to the meaning of the art of the Middle Ages; and to the meaning of what the art of the nineteenth century connoted in the lives of the people.
[8]Morris, *Signs of Change*, pp. 123-24.

the discovery about the same time that he could write poetry himself. The idea of taking orders was pushed farther and farther into the background as art and literature more and more asserted themselves in his life.

How complete this secularization was may be gathered from the fact that Morris, in his early college days, had seriously thought of using his large inheritance to found a monastery, the brotherhood to be composed of the Oxford group of high-minded young enthusiasts with whom he had been associated. He and his circle had doubtless been influenced by communities of a like nature which had been recently established in other parts of the country. Street, the renowned Gothic architect, for example, had been much interested in founding a monastery for the study and practice of religious art. By the end of 1855, however, the religious ideal in the soul of Morris had been replaced by the social ideal. Two of the group, Price and Faulkner, had become absorbingly interested in the problems of the day, and had acquired an intimate knowledge of the terrible social conditions actually existing in the large cities of England. These two became fired with zeal to reform factory conditions, to improve sanitation in the housing of the poor; and, in general, to secure the fundamental essentials of a decent life for the workers. "Things were at their worst," wrote Price, "in the forties and fifties. There was no protection for the mill-hand or miner,—no amusements but prize-fighting, dog-fighting, cock-fighting, and drinking. When a little boy, I saw many prize-fights, bestial scenes; at one a combatant was killed. The country was going to hell apace. At Birmingham a considerable section of the upper boys were quite awake to the crying evils of the period; social reform was a common topic of conversation. We were nearly all day boys, and we could not make short cuts to school without passing through slums of shocking squalor and misery, and often coming across incredible scenes of debauchery and brutality. I remember one Saturday night walking five miles from Birmingham into the Black Country, and in the last three miles I counted more than thirty lying dead drunk on the ground, nearly half of them women."[9]   Knowledge of conditions such as these, together with a knowledge of the material which this enthusiastic young group studied and talked over, inevitably led the members to the conclusion that civilization, with all that this word implies of freedom, art, and morality is conditioned by the physical and social well-being of the masses, and that the civilization which leaves out of account that physical and social well-being, is not worthy of the name. The conclusion reached was not immediately dynamic in the life of Morris, but it was strong enough to compel him to live in the actualities of the present and in dreams of the future betterment of society, rather than in the peaceful detachment of monastic life.

One of the first results of the widened and more human-hearted view of life which the Brotherhood, as the group now named itself, had come to hold in its dissatisfaction of the age, was the publishing of a magazine of a high order which was to embody the new beliefs of the members and to assist in the crusade of Carlyle and Ruskin.   The magazine was to be no temporary thing, of course; it was intended to take a place with the leading periodicals of England.   The first number appeared on New Year's Day.   But in spite of the good resolutions made when it was founded, for various reasons it lived only twelve months.   Burne-Jones wrote thus youthfully of its discontinuance: "The *Magazine* is going to smash; let it go!   The world is not converted and never will be."[10]   The publication, during its short existence, was filled each month with essays, tales, poetry, and notices of books.   Morris contributed to it material of various kinds.   Besides romances and poetry, he wrote for the February number an article on Amiens Cathedral which shows both his accurate knowledge of, and his deep interest in the Gothic architecture of France.   "I thought," he said, "that even if I could say nothing else about these grand churches, I could at

[9]Mackail, I, 64-65.
[10]Mackail, I, 108.

least tell how I loved them.   For I will say here that I think these same churches of North France the grandest, the most beautiful, the kindest, the most loving of all the buildings that the earth has ever borne."[11]

In the summer of 1855, before the new magazine was launched, some of the members of the Brotherhood took a walking-tour through Normandy.   While on this tour, Morris and Burne-Jones at last arrived at the definite conclusion that they would henceforth devote their lives to art.   To this end they resolved to give up studying for the church and agreed to leave Oxford as soon as possible.   Burne-Jones decided that he would be a painter; and Morris, that he would be an architect. Morris's decision to study architecture was the logical outcome of all of the influences and tendencies of his youth, for to Morris architecture had a wider signification than is usually accorded the term.   For him it included all of the arts of life and man; it touched, in his understanding of it, in an almost unlimited way, all of the other specific arts.

Morris lost as little time as possible in putting his new resolution into operation, although he encountered some distressing opposition from his family, which had always planned on his entering the Church. His family felt in addition that he was lowering his position in life by becoming an architect.   His mother refused at first to take her son seriously.   In a letter written during his last term at Oxford in which he delicately, but firmly stated his purpose, he wrote that the profession of architect is one that he had often thought of with longing; and if he were not permitted to follow it, he could not tell what to take up because he felt thoroughly that his chances of success and his hopes of happiness depended on doing what he liked, no matter how much drudgery might be connected with it.   He begged the friends at home not to be too much disappointed at his choice, nor to think less of him because he had changed his mind, for he did not by any means intend to give up the things he had thought of for the bettering of the world.   And

[11]Mackail, I, 96.

although he did not hope to be great in anything, he did hope to be happy in his work.[12] The opposition which his family offered to his change of purpose was not lasting, however, for in January, 1856, Morris entered the office of Street, the Gothic architect, then residing in Oxford. For some time he applied himself heart and soul to his new profession. But with characteristic energy he used his leisure moments in working with his hands in clay-modelling, carving in wood and stone, and in illuminating.

In the meantime, Burne-Jones had met Rossetti and had begun to paint under his direction. Burne-Jones' connection with Rossetti naturally brought Morris in contact with the eminent artist. To know Rossetti well was to fall under the influence of his over-mastering personality. His well-known and novel idea was that all who could, should forthwith become painters; and all who could not, should without delay buy the pictures he and other artists painted. He lost no time, therefore, in arousing Morris's enthusiastic interest in the art of painting. In the case of Morris he found his task easy, for the young student of architecture was already an ardent admirer of the Pre-Raphaelite School. In a letter of July, 1856, the new influence at work upon Morris is clearly evident.

I have seen Rossetti twice since I saw the last of you; spent almost a whole day with him the last time, last Monday, that was. . . . Rossetti says I ought to paint; he says I shall be able; now as he is a very great man, and speaks with authority and not as the scribes, I *must* try. I don't hope much, I must say, yet will try my best—he gave me practical advice on the subject. . . . So I am going to try, not giving up architecture, but trying if it is possible to get six hours a day for drawing besides office work. One won't get much enjoyment out of life at this rate, I know well, but that don't matter: I have no right to ask for it at all events— love and work, these two things only. . . . I can't enter into politico-social subjects with any interest, for on the whole I see that things are in a muddle, and I have no power or vocation to set them right in ever so little a degree. My work is the embodiment of dreams in one form or another. . . .

[12]Mackail, I, 83-85.

Yet I shall have enough to do, if I actually master this art of painting. I dare scarcely think failure possible at times, and yet I know in my mind that my chances are slender; I am glad that I am compelled to try anyhow; I was slipping off into a kind of small (very small) Palace of Art.[13]

Morris actually followed out the study of both architecture and painting for some time, working in Street's office in the day-time and going with Burne-Jones to a life school every night.   The impulse toward becoming a painter was strengthened by a visit which he made with Street the same autumn to the Netherlands; and under the new influence he gave up the study of architecture to devote himself exclusively to painting.

Better to follow out his changed plans, Morris and Burne-Jones took three unfurnished rooms together in Red Lion Square. The seemingly insignificant fact that these rooms were unfurnished prepared the way for a revolution in household decoration and household arts.   For out of this small circumstance grew Morris's later work as a manufacturer and decorator.   The two young men naturally enough began a diligent search for furnishings which would express their tastes.   Immediately they were brought face to face with the vulgarity and degradation of the decorative arts in the Victorian age.   Historians of the art of the period describe it as the lowest in the annals of the household arts.   Aymer Vallance wrote of it as follows:

There is but slight necessity to enumerate the horrors proper to the early Victorian period—the Berlin woolwork and the bead mats; the crochet antimacassars upon horse-hair sofas; the wax flowers under glass shades; the monstrosities in stamped brass and gilded stucco; chairs, tables, and other furniture hideous with veneer and curly distortions; the would-be naturalistic vegetable-patterned carpets with false shadows and misplaced perspective; and all the despicable legion of mean shams and vulgarities which have been exposed and held up to ridicule times without number. The memory of them, associated as it is indissolubly with the geranium and crinoline, must be only too painfully vivid to the minds of many of us.   It is sufficient to say that love nor money could not procure beautiful objects of contemporary manufacture for any purpose of household furnishing or adornment when William

[13]Mackail, I, 106-07.

Morris undertook the Herculean and seemingly hopeless task of decorative reform, and wrought and brought deliverance from the thraldom of the ugly, which oppressed all the so-called arts of this country.[14]

Morris and Burne-Jones thought that they had solved the problem of household decoration and furnishing for themselves when they decided that since they could not buy furnishings to their taste, they would make designs and have them executed. But the solution was not so easy of attainment. They found to their amazement that the manufacturers could not do satisfactory work even though good designs were given to them. They were finally obliged to trust their designs to a carpenter in the neighborhood over whom they watched while he was at work. Rossetti, who described the resulting productions as "intensely mediaeval", provided designs for paintings on the panels of the cupboard and the sides of the settle. The wardrobe was decorated with paintings by Burne-Jones from *The Prioress's Tale* of Chaucer.

Morris, happy and comfortable in his new environment, worked at painting with the tremendous energy and enthusiasm which always characterized his work. He discovered about this time his remarkable gift of pattern designing; and this discovery, coupled with the knowledge that though he could do creditable work in painting, he could never attain the proficiency that he desired in the drawing of animate forms, induced him to give up his recently-born ambition to become a painter of pictures, and in its place to take up the work of a designer of patterns and a decorator. At last, after much change of purpose and wavering, but always, it must be remembered, within the sacred precincts of art, Morris had found his true vocation. But he did not at once drop his brush; Rossetti had a task for him. Rossetti, with colossal assurance, had accepted for himself and for his friends the work of decorating the new University Museum at Oxford, the paintings to be de-

[14]Aymer Vallance, *William Morris, His Art*, etc., p. 55. See also Walter Crane's article on Morris in *Scribner's*, 22, 88 ff.

signed and carried out under his direction. Morris worked rapidly and energetically at his assignment and consequently had his picture begun before any of the others had even made their drawings. Although the famous plan of decoration ended in failure, it had the result of bringing Morris into a greater intimacy with the Pre-Raphaelite artists.

For the next year and longer Morris lived in Oxford, still diligently keeping on with his painting, but at the same time trying his hand at other arts: carving, drawing, coloring designs for stained glass windows, modelling in clay, and even embroidering. During this year also he composed poems for his volume of poetry published in 1858, entitled *The Defence of Guenevere and Other Poems*. As was natural and indeed inevitable, Morris's first volume of poems is dominated by the spirit of the Middle Ages. The poignant charm and the haunting sadness of the old world lie over them; romance is written on every page. But the poems received very little notice from the literary world or from the public. Tennyson was at his height; it could not be otherwise.

This same year at Oxford, marked for Morris by much groping, wavering, and discovery, was further eventful in that he met Jane Burden, who the next year became his wife. With the building of Red House, as it was called, which Morris prepared for his bride, a new chapter opened in the life and activity of William Morris. He was now twenty-five years old, with all the tendencies of his youthful character crystallized into habits. Mackail describes him thus:

The Bohemian life in London had by this time raised Morris's unconventionality, which had always been extreme, to a still more excessive height. To wear long hair, and a soft felt hat, and to smoke a pipe in season and out of season, was still, as in the earlier days of Clive Newcome, the mark of the artist. But Morris exceeded even the customary license of Gandish. "Morris went to Jones' on Sunday night," runs a note in Miss Price's diary, "while they were here; and his hair was so long and he looked so wild that the servant who opened the door would not let him in, thinking he was a burglar." He forswore dress-clothes, and there is a ludicrous story of his ineffectual attempt to get into Hughes' evening trousers when he was going to dine at high table in Christ Church.

To go into society was a torture to him, and he never took pains to conceal it.   One of the tribulations of these months was the task equally hard in either case, of evading or accepting the invitation of Dr. Henry Acland, whose intimacy with Ruskin and appreciation of the Pre-Raphaelite school led him to offer constant hospitality to the young painters.   Once, when they were to dine with Dr. Acland, Morris invented an illness and sent his apologies by Burne-Jones.   Unfortunately, Burne-Jones arrived with this message when there still wanted a few minutes to dinner-time.   Acland, who was all kindness, instantly, to Burne-Jones' infinite dismay, put on his hat and went around to see the sick man in his lodgings; he was found, apparently in the best of health and spirits, sitting at dinner with Faulkner and playing cribbage over the meal.   He had to confess recovery and be led off to dinner.   Another story of the same period is characteristic.   At dinner one evening in George Street, Prinsep said something, whether intentionally or not, which offended Morris.   Everyone expected an outburst of fury.   But by a prodigious effort of self-control, Morris swallowed his anger, and only bit his fork,—one of the common, four-pronged, fiddle-pattern kind,—which was crushed and twisted almost beyond recognition.[15]

The William Morris here described, caring nothing for conventionalities or fashions, always knowing just what he liked without an instant's hesitation, a man of marked individuality, gusty temper, with wide capacities for sympathy, survived in the William Morris of later years, unchanged except for the immeasurable gift of an added grasp on the significance of life, and a noble purpose to make life, if possible, worthy of men.   But at twenty-five, Morris had no definite hope, no definite purpose to attack the commercial life of the nineteenth century. The work of Owen and of the Christian Socialists had apparently passed him by on the other side.   His aim at this time was rather to do as much as he could in redeeming the architectural arts from ugliness and vulgarity.   The wider social outlook was not yet his. The seeds of a great human-heartedness, which were to make of him a man of broader vision, thinking and feeling in cycles for the good of humanity, instead of in the meagre span of man's threescore years and ten, were, however, already sown.   He was on the way towards carrying out his purpose to secure to every man a man's share of what goes on in life.

[15]Mackail, I, 128.   Noyes, p. 20, discounts the story of the fork.

CHAPTER II

THE RED HOUSE AND THE FIRM

It has been said that all of Morris's work as a decorative manufacturer began with the building of Red House; but it is more accurate to say that it began with the furnishing of the rooms at Red Lion Square. The new home which Morris planned and furnished for his bride was certainly the result of his activity thus far in art. As might be expected, the dwelling was a decided departure from "square-box-with-a-lid" style prevailing in residence architecture. It was built in the shape of an L with an oak staircase in the angle. The large drawing-room, located on the upper floor, Morris declared he meant to make the most beautiful in England. Although the room was never finished as he conceived it, the decoration of the room went on for the five years which Morris and his family spent there. The decorative plan specified that the walls to within five feet of the floor were to be covered with a series of pictures. The subjects of the paintings were chosen from the English mediaeval romance of Sir Degrevant. Burne-Jones completed three of the panels. The five feet below the pictures was to be hung with embroidery. In fact, every room in the house was to have its special decorative scheme, depending upon the purpose of the room.

The experience at Red Lion Square had taught Morris that all of the furnishings and decorations of Red House must be especially designed and supplied to order. This was a significant fact for Morris, and indeed for the decorative arts. Out of the needs of this first home of Morris grew quite naturally the firm which later came to be known as Morris & Company. Who originated the idea of forming a company is not definitely known; but the successful conduct of the business was without doubt due to the energy, the enthusiasm, and the originality of Morris. Inclination and necessity had combined to give him ample opportunity to practice most of the domestic arts. He had made designs, he had embroidered, and he had decorated walls. The organization of the company was therefore the natural outcome of his work thus far. The various artists associated with Morris assisted in drawing up the plans for the firm. It was agreed that each of them should pay a certain sum, in addition to contributing designs for the various articles of use and ornament according to the demand for them. No profits were to be shared until each member had been paid for his designs.[1] Morris undertook the business management. At first only two men outside the firm were employed. Great pains were taken to exclude the merely commercial element; therefore it was a condition of employment that all workmen should possess more than average appreciation.

The first thing which the new firm did in starting the business was to get out a circular explaining its nature. The circular was headed "Morris, Marshall, Faulkner & Company, Fine Art Workmen in Painting, Carving, Furniture, and the Metals." The names of the eight members of the firm followed, together with a statement of the purpose and the kinds of work undertaken. The announcement of the company is significant in view of the revolution which took place in the household arts during the next few decades,[2] and significant also for the development of Morris.

The growth of Decorative art in this country, owing to the efforts of the English Architects, has now reached a point at which it seems desirable that Artists of reputation should devote their time to it. Although no doubt particular instances of success may be cited, still it must be generally felt that attempts of this kind hitherto have been crude and fragmentary. Up to this time, the want of that artistic supervision, which can alone bring about harmony between the various parts of a successful work had been increased by the necessarily excessive outlay, consequent on taking one individual artist from his pictorial labors.

The Artists whose names appear above hope by association to do away with this difficulty. Having among their number men of varied qualifications, they will be able to undertake any species of

[1]Vallance, p. 56.
[2]Walter Crane, *loc. cit.*, pp. 88 ff.

decoration, mural or otherwise, from pictures, properly so called, down to the consideration of the smallest work susceptible of art and beauty. It is anticipated that by such co-operation, the largest amount of what is essentially the artist's work, along with his constant supervision, will be secured at the smallest possible expense, while the work done must necessarily be of a much more complete order, than if any single artist were incidentally employed in the usual manner.

These Artists having for many years been deeply attached to the study of the Decorative Arts of all times and countries, have felt more than most people the want of some one place where they could obtain or get produced work of a genuine and beautiful character. They have therefore now established themselves as a firm for the production, by themselves and under their supervision, of—

I.   Mural Decoration, either in Pictures or in Pattern Work, or merely in the arrangement of Colours, as applied to dwelling-houses, churches, or public buildings.
II. Carving generally, as applied to Architecture.
III. Stained Glass, especially with reference to its harmony with Mural Decoration.
IV. Metal Work in all its branches, including Jewellery.
V.   Furniture, either depending for its beauty on its own design, on the application of materials hitherto overlooked, or on its conjunction with Figure and Pattern Painting. Under this head is included Embroidery of all kinds, Stamped Leather, and ornamental work in other such materials, besides every article necessary for domestic use.

It is only requisite to state further, that work of all the above classes will be estimated for, and executed in a business-like manner, and it is believed that good decoration, involving rather the luxury of taste than the luxury of costliness, will be found to be much less expensive than is generally supposed.[3]

Among its rival manufacturers the announcement of the new firm naturally caused great excitement. The promoters were severely ridiculed, but the company survived the storm of jealousy and grew in spite of all hostility.[4] The year following its formation the members exhibited furniture, tapestry, and stained glass at the International Exhibition of 1862 in London, and received a medal in recognition of their work. This award aroused more and fiercer opposition from rival firms. But Morris & Company continued to thrive.

[3]Mackail, I, 150-52.
[4]Vallance, pp. 58-59.

At first their work was mainly the decoration of churches, especially providing stained-glass windows; and other branches were gradually added.   Morris made his first design for wall-paper in 1862, to be followed in after years by an almost incredible number of designs of ever-increasing artistic value.   The firm later supplied tiles, chintzes, and carpets.

Such was the success of the Company that by 1865 the business had so increased that it was found necessary to move into larger quarters.   A severe illness, caused by exposure in riding from London to Red House at Bexley Heath, as well as greater responsibility in connection with the firm, brought Morris at last, though most reluctantly, to resolve upon giving up the beautiful home into which he and his artist-friends had put many days of thought and work, and in which they together had spent many congenial hours.   The decision once taken, Red House and all of its immovable art treasures were soon sold.   Morris and his family moved to Queen Square, Bloomsbury, which remained the place of their residence and the place of Morris's work for seventeen years.

Relieved of the necessity of travelling back and forth to London, and with business affairs on a firm footing, Morris found leisure, in addition to his management of the company, for the writing of poetry.   *The Life and Death of Jason* was published in 1867, and the first volume of *The Earthly Paradise* in 1868.

That Morris had not forgotten that the world needed betterment may be traced, though in no marked way and with no hint of a definite purpose in mind, in some of his poetry of this period, seemingly remote as it is in subject-matter from modern life.   It cannot be shown that in it he criticized society in any constructive or destructive way.   At this time his feelings and thoughts on social problems were in a somewhat nebulous state, held in solution, as it were, in his consciousness.   Apparently he had no more sharply defined purpose than that he would do all in his power to improve the industrial arts.   Nevertheless it is evident that the turmoil and the clash of life with all the ugliness and misery attendant upon living were deeply impressed upon his mind. "A dreamer of dreams, the idle singer of an empty day", he invites his readers in the Prologue to *The Earthly Paradise* to

> Forget six counties overhung with smoke,
> Forget the snorting steam and piston stroke,
> Forget the spreading of the hideous town;
> Think rather of the pack-horse on the down,
> And dream of London, small and white and clean,
> The clear Thames bordered by its garden green.[5]

Without doubt it is the England of Chaucer's day, the century of his country's life and art which Morris liked best to dream about and think upon that he asks us to view. Many an ancient hall, and with it the happy life its architecture expressed, is described during the progress of the poem in illuminating phrase:

> Noble the house was, nor seemed built for war,
> But rather like the work of other days,
> When men, in better peace than now they are,
> Had leisure on the world around to gaze,
> And noted well the past times changing ways;
> And fair with sculptured stories was it wrought.[6]

Portraits of a peaceful, happy king and his therefore peaceful, happy subjects speak plainly of Morris's ideals of what man's life on earth should be:

> King Admetus sat
> Among his people, wearied in such wise
> By hopeful toil as makes a paradise
> Of the rich earth; for light and far away
> Seemed all the labor of the coming day.
> And no man wished for more than then he had,
> Nor with another's mourning was made glad.

And in another tale,

> A happy man was he; no vain desire
> Of foolish fame had set his heart afire;
> No care he has the ancient bound to change,
> Nor yet for him must idle soldiers range
> From place to place about the burdened land,

[5]Morris, *The Earthly Paradise*, I, 3.
[6]Morris, *The Earthly Paradise*, I, 325.

Or thick upon the ruined corn-fields stand;
For him no trumpets blessed the bitter war
Wherein the right and wrong so mingled are,
That hardly can the man of single heart
Amid the sickening turmoil choose his part;
For him sufficed the changes of the year,
The god-sent terror was enough of fear
For him; enough the battle with the earth,
The autumn triumph over drought and dearth.
Better to him than wolf-moved battered shields
O'er poor dead corpses, seemed the stubble fields
Danced down beneath the moon, until the night
Grew dreamy with a shadowy sweet delight.

      · · · · ·

But to this king, fair Ceres' gifts, the days
Whereon men sing in flushed Lyaens' praise
Praise of old time, the bloodless sacrifice
Unto the goddess of the downcast eyes
And soft persuading lips, the ringing lyre
Unto the bearer of the holy fire
Who once had been amongst them—things like these
Seemed meet to him men's yearnings to appease,
These were the triumphs of the peaceful king.[7]

The tales in *The Earthly Paradise* abound with passages such as these just quoted. Although they show merely the bent of Morris's thoughts, yet they are significant; for they point, however lightly, to his future activities.

The following year Morris completed *The Earthly Paradise*, and took up the study of Icelandic,—a subject in which he became deeply interested. Indeed, not a great while elapsed before he began to translate sagas into English. Poetry, translation, and the direction of the firm apparently still left room for the practice of another art,—that of illuminating. He had long been interested in the art of illuminating books, and early had produced work which excited the admiration of all of his friends both for its faithful rendering of the mediaeval spirit and for its marvelous mastery of color. His early work in this field could be criticized only from the point of view of drawing; but when he again took up the art in 1870, he set about diligently to overcome this

[7]Morris, *The Earthly Paradise*, I, 331.

defect. It is almost unnecessary to add that he was completely successful.

About this time Morris began to look around him for a country house for his family. By good fortune, as he deemed it, he found Kelmscott Manor, in Oxfordshire. This house continued to be his summer home for twenty-five years. He loved the house and its surroundings with what really amounted to an intense passion, as he loved everything that appeared "to guard the fairness of the earth." This passion he voiced again and again in his writings. For example, even in his Utopia, where all is transcendently beautiful, he would not be without Kelmscott Manor just as it was in the nineteenth century. One passage is particularly interesting to the student of Morris's philosophy of life and of his theory of architecture:

... We crossed the road, and my hand raised the latch of a door in the wall, and we stood presently on a stone path which led up to the old house. The garden between the wall and the house was redolent of the June flowers, and the roses were rolling over one another with that delicious superabundance of small, well-tended gardens which at first sight takes away all thought save that of beauty. The black-birds were singing their loudest, the doves were cooing on the roof-ridge, the rooks in the high-elm trees beyond were garrulous among the young leaves, and the swifts wheeled whining about the gables. And the house itself was a fit guardian for all the beauty of this heart of summer.

O me! O me! How I love the earth, the seasons, and the weather and all things that deal with it, and all that grows out of it—as this has done! If I could but say or show how I love it![8]

A house that I love; with a reasonable love I think; for though my words may give you no idea of any special charm about it, yet I assure you the charm is there; so much has the old house grown up out of the soil and the lives of those that lived on it; some thin thread of tradition, a half-anxious sense of the delight of meadow and acre and wood and river; a certain amount (not too much let us hope) of commonsense; a liking for making materials serve one's turn, and perhaps at bottom some little grain of sentiment:—this I think was what went to the making of the old place.[9]

Absorbed as Morris was in many things, he found time to plan a journey to Iceland, which he took the

[8]Morris, *News From Nowhere*, etc., pp. 201-3.
[9]Mackail, I, 231.

following year. Its old sagas, its romantic history, and its simple life made Iceland the most attractive country on the earth to him. In the tales of its heroes he thought he found something which answered to his own desires of what man's life on earth should mean. The terrible wastes with their terrible mountains, the very savagery of the landscape made so lasting an impression on his imagination that many years later traces of the influence of his journey may be found in the descriptive parts of his writings.[10]

Immediately upon his return from Iceland, Morris began work upon the last long poem which he produced for several years,—*Love is Enough*, a poem which suggests vaguely the mediaeval moralities. He intended to have the little volume decorated, and to that purpose designed and cut on wood the borders for the pages and the illustrations. But, as had been the case with *The Earthly Paradise*, which he had also planned to decorate with specially designed borders and suitable illustrations, he found that he could not get his designs executed. The age had apparently lost the art of making beautiful books, as well as many other arts. The reason why was always teasing Morris's mind. The questioning bore fruit later.

For a time,—for these were restless years,—Morris was absorbed in the affairs of his business and in the production of artistic wares. In 1873 he made a journey to Italy, but Italy pleased him little. He found himself entirely out of sympathy with the art of the later Renaissance, and with but little interest for the art of the earlier period. He regarded the Renaissance, so fruitful for modern life in many of its phases, as a blight to art; in this field he believed that it had no claim to the title of "The New Birth". For Morris regarded the glorious artists of the Renaissance as the result of the old, not the product of a new order of things. In Art, the New Birth meant almost entirely the looking back to older days.

[10]Mackail, I, 240 ff.

Art by no means stood still in those later days of the Renaissance,"
he wrote, "but took the downward road with terrible swiftness,
and tumbled down at the bottom of the hill, where, as if bewitched,
it lay long in great content, believing itself to be the art of Michael
Angelo, while it was the art of men whom nobody remembers
but those who want to sell their pictures. . . . When the great
masters of the Renaissance were gone, they, who stung by the
desire of doing something new, turned their mighty hands to the
work of destroying the last remains of living popular art, putting
in its place for awhile the results of their own wonderful individuality—when these great men were dead, the lesser men of the
ordinary type were masquerading in their garments; then at last
it was seen what the so-called new birth really was; then we could
see that it was the fever of the strong man yearning to accomplish
something before his death, not the simple hope of the child who
has long years of life and growth before him.[11]

Morris was firmly convinced that the Renaissance
had destroyed the art of building in Italy.   St. Peter's
at Rome was an example to him of that destruction,
"the very type of pride and tyranny, of all that crushes
out the love of art in simple people, and makes art a toy
of little estimation for the idle hours of the rich and
cultivated.   Between that time and this, art has been
shut up in a prison."[12]

As Morris thought about the problem of the significance of art in the life of the people and in the life of the
nation, ideas sown in his mind years ago by the study
of Carlyle and of Ruskin, and by his association with
the young Oxford students of the Brotherhood, all of
whom had the notion of doing great things for the world,
began to show signs of active life.   In a letter written
on March 24, 1874, definite evidence of awakening
appears, and with it something like a definite ideal of
the sort of life men should have the opportunity to live.
He did not yet feel called, however, to the vocation of
the social reformer.

   . . . Monday was a day here to set one longing to get away;
as warm as June; yet the air heavy as it often is in England; though
the town looks rather shocking on such days, and then instead of
the sweet scents, one gets an extra smell of dirt.   Surely if people
lived five hundred years instead of threescore and ten, they would

[11]Morris, *Hopes and Fears for Art*, pp. 80-81.
[12]Morris, *Architecture, Industry and Wealth*, p. 4.

find some better way of living than in such a sordid loathsome place, but now it seems to be nobody's business to try to better things—isn't mine you see, in spite of all my grumbling—but look, suppose people lived in little communities among gardens and green fields, so that you could be in the country in five minutes' walk, and had few wants, almost no furniture for instance, and no servants, and studied the (difficult) arts of enjoying life, and finding out what they really wanted; then I think one might hope civilization had really begun. But as it is, the best thing one can wish for this country at least is, meseems, some great and tragical circumstances, so that if they cannot have pleasant life, which is what one means by civilization, they may at least have a history and something to think of—all of which won't happen in our time. Sad grumbling—but do you know, I have got to go to a wedding next Tuesday; and it enrages me to think that I lack courage to say, I don't care for either of you, and you neither of you care for me, and I won't waste a day out of my precious life grinning a company grin at you two.[13]

Another letter of Morris's written the following autumn shows the same frame of mind slightly intensified.

I would like you to understand as well as my clumsy letter-writing will let you, how very happy I was these few days in the north. I hope you will let me come again some time; and that then you will think me less arrogant on the what shall I say?—Wesleyan-tradesman-unsympathetic-with-art-subjects than you seemed to think me the other day; though indeed I don't accuse myself of it either; but I think to shut one's eyes to ugliness and vulgarity is wrong, even when they show themselves in people not inhuman. Do you know, when I see a poor devil drunk and brutal I always feel, quite apart from my aesthetical perceptions, a sort of shame, as if I myself had some hand in it. Neither do I grudge the triumph that the modern mind finds in having made the world (or a small corner of it) quieter and less violent, but I think that this blindness to beauty will draw down a kind of revenge one day: who knows? Years ago men's minds were full of art and the dignified shows of life, and they had but little time for justice and peace; and the vengeance on them was not increase of the violence they did not heed, but destruction of the art they heeded. So perhaps the gods are preparing troubles and terrors for the world (or our small corner of it) again, that it may once again become beautiful and dramatic withal; for I do not believe they will have it dull and ugly forever. Meantime, what is good enough for them must content us; though sometimes I should like to know why the story of the earth gets so unworthy.[14]

[13]Mackail, I, 302-03.
[14]Mackail, I, 304-05.

The reason why the story of the earth grows so unworthy became increasingly clear to Morris in these
days of active and purposeful pondering.   And the deeper
he sought for causes, the more it became his conviction
that it was his duty to endeavor in some positive way
to make the life of man on earth more worthy.

The years of the middle seventies were as crowded
with diverse occupations as had been the years of the
sixties.   A second journey to Iceland in July, 1873,
had stimulated him to write more Icelandic stories.   A
translation of the Aeneid followed; and in the meantime
he worked busily at learning to dye in order that the
firm might add another useful art to its already long
list.   The art of dyeing, Morris discovered, like all
other of the household arts, was in a very sad condition.
It was almost impossible to get material which would
take dyes properly, or to get dyeing done which would
be durable.   He therefore gave liberally of his super-
abundant stock of energy to the study of the theory
and the art of dyeing from its most ancient beginnings
on record.   But even while deeply absorbed in mastering a new industrial art, he still found time to work on
the composition of *Sigurd the Volsung*, a poem which he
had dreamed of writing ever since he had published his
translation of *The Volsunga Saga* in 1870.   *Sigurd the
Volsung* was published in 1876.   "This is the great
Story of the North," wrote Morris on one occasion,
"which should be to all our race what the Tale of Troy
was to the Greeks; to all our race, first, and afterwards,
when the change of the world has made our race nothing
more than a name of what has been; a story, too, then
should it be to those that come after us no less than the
Tale of Troy has been to us."[15]

With the adoration of Courage in the face of doom
which Morris found to be the basic stone of the philosophy of the Northmen, he always had the greatest
sympathy.   In a way he accepted it as his own and
made it the message of his great epic to his times.   These
ancestors of ours held a vital belief, one which he was

[15]Mackail, I, 330.

never weary of praising. "It may be that the world shall worsen," said Morris in a restatement of the belief of the North,

that men shall grow afraid to "change their life", that the world shall be weary itself and sicken, and none but faint-hearts be left—who knows? So at any rate comes the end at last, and the Evil, bound for awhile, is loose, and all nameless merciless horrors that on earth we figure by fire and earthquake and venom and ravin. So comes the great strife: and like the kings and heroes that they loved, here also must the Gods die, the Gods who made that strifeful imperfect earth, not blindly indeed, yet foredoomed. One by one they extinguish for ever some dread and misery that all this time has brooded over life, and one by one, their work accomplished, they die; till at last the great destruction breaks out over all things, and the old earth and heavens are gone, and then a new heaven and earth. What goes on then? Who shall say of us who know only rest and peace by toil and strife? And what shall be our share of it? Well, sometimes we needs must think that we shall live again: yet if that were not, would it not be enough that we helped to make this unnameable glory, and lived not altogether deedless? Think of the joy we have in praising great men, and how we turn their stories over and over, and fashion their lives for our joy; and this also we ourselves may give to the world.

This seems to me pretty much the religion of the Northmen. I think one would be a happy man if one could hold it, in spite of the wild dreams and the dreadful imaginings that hung about it here and there.[16]

[16]Mackail, I, 333-34.

CHAPTER III

Public and political activities engaged Morris in 1876-77. For twenty years previous he had by his earnest work in the industrial arts defended life against barbarism; his participation now in politics and in public affairs was but another attack from a different angle upon the same citadel. His interest in public life, let it be emphasized, was not the sudden aberration of the artist and literary man; it was the inevitable result of his temperament and development,—a development which can be traced at least from the time he went up to Oxford in 1853 with the intention of entering the Church. There, as has been pointed out, in the association of the group of young idealists gathered about him and Burne-Jones, under the awakening influence of Carlyle and Ruskin, Morris's ideals expanded from the monastic to the social ideal of service. In the first flush of this new widening of ideals, the *Oxford and Cambridge Magazine* was founded. A significant step in Morris's career was taken,—for which his whole life had been prepangi,—rwhen on his first journey through Northern France, he and Burne-Jones made the resolution henceforth to devote their lives to art, though Morris, as he told his mother, did not altogether give up the dreams he had had for the betterment of the world.[1] By the honest, sincere, and conscientious work which he did in the industrial arts, the progress of which can be traced year by year throughout his life, and of which the result, on the whole, is so great that he is said to have changed the appearance of half the houses in London and substituted art for ugliness all over the kingdom,[2] he did an immeasurable amount for the betterment of the world. Yet this period of his life must be called passive and his work of indirect

[1]Mackail, I, 83-86.
[2]Vallance, p. 144.

influence compared with his active and positive endeavor later to solve the social problem as he saw it.

Morris's entrance into public affairs was made from
two opposite directions: through his activity for the
protection of ancient buildings; and through his interest
in the Eastern Question. He was the founder of the
Society for the Protection of Ancient Buildings. From
its inception in 1876 to the end of his life, he served on
its committees, traveled about the country to inspect
buildings for the Society, and lectured and wrote unceasingly for the cause it upheld.[3] Ruskin's impas-
sioned pleading for the ancient monuments of art probably first directed Morris's attention to this subject.
No cause but one was dearer to Morris's heart than
that of saving the venerable buildings of England and
of the Continent both from careless neglect and from so-
called "restoration". In several instances buildings
had been restored by one architect only to have the
work of the first restorer destroyed by a second who
thought his ideas to be nearer the ancient forms. The
result of such treatment to buildings which were works
of art and monuments of history was undeniably fatal.
Both Morris and Ruskin pleaded for care in the preservation of the buildings and monuments intact. Morris
especially urged waiting, in the belief that if his opinions
concerning restoration were found to be wrong, the
buildings would always be there to restore; but if he
were right,—and he really had no doubt of his position,
— the ancient art, once destroyed, could never be brought
to life again.[4]

The principles of the society for the Protection of
Ancient Buildings were drawn up by Morris in 1877.
In substance they bring out the point that the last
fifty years of attention to the antiquities of England
and of Europe had done more for their destruction than
all of the foregoing centuries of revolution, violence,
and contempt. The failure of modern restoration
he ascribed to the death of architecture as a pop-

[3]Vallance, p. 275.
[4]Morris, *Hopes and Fears for Art*, pp. 99 ff.

ular art; and the nineteenth century, though it had much knowledge of the styles of other centuries, had no style of its own.   Because architecture had been a subject of study, contemporary builders believed that ancient buildings could be restored to their former state by stripping off decaying and broken-down parts, and substituting in their places work purporting to be the same in spirit and design as the work of mediaeval days. This, Morris declared, is a strange and fatal idea which "implies that it is possible to strip from a building this, that, and the other part of its history,—of its life, that is,—and then stay the hand at some arbitrary point, and leave it still historical, living, and even as it was." In the earlier times when a building needed restoration or repairs, no such forgeries were practiced, either because knowledge was lacking to the restorers, or because instinct kept them from desecration.   When changes or repairs were necessary, they were made in the fashion of the time, and were therefore eloquent of the spirit of the age in which they were wrought.   The result of this policy was that a building might show many changes, some visible and even harsh, but nevertheless interesting and instructive by their very contrast.   The repairs or changes were not, at any rate, misleading.   They were done honestly, without any intention to make the work appear as if it had been executed a century or centuries before.   In our age, however, the builders attempt to restore after the ancient style; but since there is no architectural tradition animating the workmen, they work each according to his individual caprice. In the attempt to copy the style of a former age and to imagine what earlier craftsmen would or might have done, they necessarily tamper with the ancient art, thus destroying altogether the appearance of antiquity of such parts as are left, and also the value of the old monuments as historical documents.   Most of the larger minsters and a still larger number of smaller and less pretentious buildings had already been thus destroyed both in England and on the Continent.   Morris pleaded earnestly with the public not to permit such restoration, but instead to protect the ancient architecture. He urged that the old buildings be propped up in order to stave off decay by every means possible, and begged that no pretence be resorted to by putting art work in the place of the decaying parts. In the case of buildings which had become inconvenient or unsafe for their present use, he advised the erection of others instead of the altering or making stable of the old. In a word, he wished our ancient buildings to be regarded "as monuments of a bygone art, created by bygone manners that modern art cannot meddle with without destroying. Thus, and thus only shall we escape the reproach of our learning being turned into a snare to us; thus, and thus only, can we protect our ancient buildings and hand them down instructive and venerable to those that come after us."[5]

Morris set on foot operations in 1879 to deter the Minister of Public Works in Italy from allowing the proposed restoration of St. Marks. In an address before the Society he urged upon the members and all lovers of art the importance of leaving the cathedral alone, reminding them that there was but one St. Marks, and that it belonged not to Venice only, but to the whole world.[6] Great mischief had already been done it by two previous restorations: Morris has the credit of having prevented a third.[7] But not only did Morris plead for the preservation of St. Marks; his words were no less earnest for the monuments of his own country. In his lecture on *Pattern Designing*, speaking of the homes and the churches of our forefathers, he said:

Here in the land we yet love, they built their homes and temples; if not so majestically as many peoples have done, yet in such sweet accord with the familiar nature amidst which they dwelt, that when by some happy chance we come across the work they wrought, untouched by any but natural change, it fills us with a satisfying, untroubled happiness that few things else could bring us. Must our necessities destroy, must our restless ambition mar the source of this innocent pleasure, which rich and poor may share alike,

[5]Vallance, pp. 274-75.
[6]Morris, *Hopes and Fears for Art*, p. 95.
[7]Vallance, p. 282.

this communion with the very hearts of departed men? Must we sweep away these touching memories of our stout forefathers and their troublous days, that won our present peace and liberties? If our necessities compel us to it, I say we are an unhappy people; if our vanity lure us into it, I say we are a foolish and light-minded people, who have not the wits to take a little trouble to avoid spoiling our own goods. Yes, the goods of the people of England, now and in time to come; we who are now alive are but life-renters of them. Any of us who pretend to any culture know well that, in destroying or injuring one of these buildings, we are destroying the pleasure, the culture, in a word, the humanity of unborn generations. . . . I say such destruction is an act of brutal dishonesty. . . . I think the poor remains of our ancient buildings in themselves, as memorials of history and works of art are worth more than any temporary use they can be put to. . . . In days to come people will feel ashamed of us that we took so little trouble to guard the things they have heard told of as so precious; that we could not exercise something more of patience and forethought in arranging the relative claims of what our lives compelled us to make for our immediate use, and what our honor and gratitude bade us hand down from our fathers to our children. . . . I love art, and I love history, but it is living art and living history that I love. . . . It is in the interest of living art and living history that I oppose so-called restoration. What history can there be in a building bedaubed with ornament, which cannot at the best be anything but a hopeless and lifeless imitation of the hope and vigor of the earlier world?[8]

. . . In these days, when history is studied so keenly through the original documents and has thereby gained a vitality which makes it such a contrast to the dull, and not too veracious accounts of kings and nobles that used to do duty for history, it seems pitiable indeed that the most important documents of all, the ancient buildings of the Middle Ages, the work of the associated labor and thought of the *people*, the result of a train of tradition unbroken from the earliest ages of art, should be falsified by an uneasy desire to do something, a vulgar craving for formal completeness, which is almost essentially impossible in a building that has *grown* from decade to decade, and century to century.

Again the special beauty of mediaeval buildings, which after a long period of neglect and ignorance, has forced itself on the attention of our time, should surely now be recognized by all intelligent persons as the outcome of the conditions of the society of that epoch, a thing impossible of reproduction under the modern system of capitalist and wage-earner. . . . the whole surface of a mediaeval building shows intelligent, free, and therefore pleasurable work on

[8]Morris, *Architecture, Industry and Wealth*, pp. 334-35.

the part of the actual workman, while that of the modern building
has nothing in it more than toil done against the grain under the
threat of starvation.[9]

When the restoration of the interior of Westminster
Abbey was rumored, Morris was intensely aroused and
protested in the name of the Society against attempting
what he called so wanton and vain a project.   The building was the work, he said "of the inseparable will of a
body of men, who worked as they lived, because they
could not do otherwise, and unless you can bring these
men back from the dead, you cannot 'restore' one verse
of their epic.   Rewrite the lost trilogies of Aeschylus,
put a beginning and an end to the 'Fight at Finnsburg',
finish the Squire's tale for Chaucer, even if you cannot
          'call up him that left half-told
          The story of Cambuscan bold.'
and if you can succeed in that, you may then 'restore'
Westminster Abbey."[10]

From the work of Morris for the Society for the Protection of Ancient Buildings and for the cause it represented, grew his later activity as a lecturer and instructor
in the principles of art, and as a founder and leader of a
guild of craftsmen who exist at the present time as the
permanent result of his influence and endeavours.   The
aim of this guild of craftsmen was single: a new birth of
the decorative arts which should take into account both
the worker and the consumer.   Included in this movement was another: the reorganization of work within a
single workshop.   This meant that the manager, the
designer, and the worker or executor of the design should
no longer work apart, separated by class, by education,
and by hostility the one from the other.   The reorganization went so far as to include the coördination of the
workshops.   This was a significant movement, for it
meant the beginning of a trained organization of handicraftsmen, and the building of a school of workers with
a living tradition behind them.   Of all of this far-reach-

[9]Vallance, pp. 293-94.
[10]Morris, *Architecture and History and Westminster Abbey*, pp. 47-48.

ing and double movement, which embraces such men
as J. T. Cobden-Sanderson, Walter Crane, Heywood
Sumner, W. A. S. Benson, and in America, Elbert
Hubbard and Gustav Stickley, William Morris and
his ideas and practise were and are the inspiring and
guiding influence.[11]

Even while William Morris was engaged in taking
the first steps toward the founding of the Society for
the Protection of Ancient Buildings, he was interesting
himself in the Eastern Question Association. The immediate cause of his action in this direction is to be
found in affairs in the East, and in the influence which
they exerted in England. In 1875-76 the Serbs in
Herzegovina and the Bulgarians revolted to gain their
independence. The Turks, because of the accessibility
of the Bulgarian country, visited upon this unhappy
people the full force of a Turkish vengeance. A hundred
villages were destroyed, more than thirty thousand
people were massacred, and thousands of Christian

[11]Mackail, I, 339; II, 196 ff. See also *Philistine*, December, 1908. An announcement of *A William Morris Book* in this publication runs as follows: "An
authentic statistician claims that ninety-five per cent of all English and American
homes show the influence of William Morris. This man, master of seven trades,
socialistic philospher, worker, lover of things beautiful, taught two countries how to
furnish a house. He, Pre-Raphaelite leader, dressed as a laborer, believed in the
divinity of work, and in demanding better conditions for fellow-workingmen know-
ingly let pass his opportunity to become Poet-Laureate of England." This is very
far, to be sure, from a scientific statement of the facts of the case, but it is nevertheless interesting, if exaggerated, testimony to the influence of Morris as a craftsman.
   Another announcement savoring strongly of advertisement, yet bearing witness
to the new ideals in house decoration, is to be found in the catalogue of Gustav
Stickley, maker of well-known Craftsman furnishings in the United States. "The
Craftsman idea makes for the development in this country of an art and architecture which shall express the spirit of the American people; for the creation of conditions which shall provide the best home environment for our children; for a form
of industrial education which will enable men and women to earn their living under
all circumstances; and for more reasonable and healthful standards of life and work."
—*Craftsman Furniture*, January, 1909.
   In the *William Morris Book* which Elbert Hubbard announced in the notice
quoted above, Mr. Hubbard stated, p. 34: "To the influence of William Morris
does the civilized world owe its salvation from the mad rage and rush for the tawdry
and the cheap in home decoration. It will not do to say that if William Morris
had not called a halt, some one else would, nor to cavil by declaring that the in-
anities of the Plush-covered Age followed the Era of the Hair-cloth sofa. These
things are frankly admitted, but the refreshing fact remains that fully one-half the
homes of England and America have been influenced by the strong taste and vivid
personality of one strong, earnest, courageous man." Evidently there are no real
statistics on the number of homes actually showing the influence of William Morris's
ideas in household arts. The references are submitted for what they are worth.

women were carried off into a terrible captivity. So atrocious were the horrors inflicted by the Turks upon their victims that this chapter of history is familiar to students under the name of "Bulgarian Atrocities". Europe was so aroused by the Turkish action that the threatened armed intervention of Russia brought no immediate interference from the other Powers, although they looked with customary jealousy upon Russia's action.[12]   A few Englishmen were deeply stirred by the barbaric cruelty of the Turks, and not being particularly interested in the feeling of the English government against Russian aggression, founded the Eastern Question Association.   Morris became the treasurer of the society, and worked in the cause of justice and of humanity with the impetuous ardor characteristic of his temperament.   In a letter to Faulkner on the 15th of November, 1877, he wrote:

I am very willing to receive you as a convert if you must needs ticket yourself so, though I don't see the need, as both your views and mine being interpreted mean declaring ourselves enemies of that den of thieves, the Turkish Government.   As to the Russians, all I say is this; we *might* have acted so that they could have had no pretext for interfering with Turkey in accordance with the unanimous wish of Europe; we *have* so acted as to drive them into separate interference whatever may come; and to go to war with them for this would be a piece of outrageous injustice.   Furthermore, if we came victorious out of such a war, what would we do with Turkey, if we didn't wish to be damned?   "Take it ourselves," says the bold man, "and rule it as we rule India".   But the bold man don't live in England at present I think; and I know what the Tory trading, stock-jobbing scoundrel that one calls an Englishman today would do with it: he would shut his eyes hard over it, get his widows to lend it money, and sell it vast quantities of bad cotton.[13]

In May, 1877, Morris issued a manifesto which, as Mackail says, is significant for the tone it takes on the political action, and for the body to whom it was addressed.   It was directed "To the Working Men of England" and it exhorts them not to be hoodwinked into war with Russia by those who have nothing to

[12]C. A. Fyffe, *History of Modern Europe*, p. 1026
[13]Mackail, I, 347-48.

lose by the war, who would lead them into battle against a people not their enemies, "against freedom, against nature, against the hope of the world."

Working men of England, [the manifesto read] one word of warning yet: I doubt if you know the bitterness of hatred against freedom and progress that lies at the hearts of a certain part of the richer classes in this country: their newspapers veil it in a kind of decent language, but do but hear them talking among themselves, as I have often, and I know not whether scorn or anger would prevail in you at their folly and insolence.   These men cannot speak of your order, of its aims, of its leaders, without a sneer or an insult; these men, if they had the power (may England perish rather!), would thwart your just aspirations, and would silence you, would deliver you bound hand and foot forever to irresponsible capital.   Fellow-citizens, look to it, and if you have any wrongs to be redressed,—if you cherish your most worthy hope of raising your whole order peacefully and solidly, if you thirst for leisure and knowledge, if you long to lessen these inequalities which have been our stumbling-block since the beginning of the world, then cast aside sloth and cry out against an Unjust War, and urge us of the middle-classes to do not less.[14]

A year later when international relations became more complicated through Russia's success, and war appeared to be certain, Morris wrote on January 5, 1878: "This is terrible news.   I confess I am really astounded at the folly that can play with such tremendous tools in this way: and more and more I feel how entirely right the flattest democracy is."[15]

Certainly the words just quoted are sufficiently straightforward.   The social teachings of Carlyle and the art-doctrine of Ruskin, together with his own experience in the industrial arts, his own passionate love of beauty, which implies in his case a necessary hatred of modern civilization, and his active participation in the political problems of the hour, brought Morris at last by a direct and logical road to his democratic beliefs.   This was no sudden conversion, no temporary aberration of mind, as some apologists for this part of his career like to explain, but a gradual and natural growth and burgeoning of seed sown in his mind twenty-

[14]Mackail, I, 349-50.
[15]Mackail, I, 350.

five years before.   In the *Bellerophon of Argos*, written in 1870, Morris questions himself:

"Yea, and bethink thee, mayst thou not be born
To raise the crushed and succour the forlorn,
And in the place of sorrow to set mirth,
Gaining a great name through the wondering earth?"

Here he saw the parting of the ways; but on which to travel,—the one he had been walking thus far, or the one travelled by the conscious missionary of social reform, he did not know.   In later years, after Morris had joined a Socialist organization, he said in a lecture delivered at Oxford that he had once hoped that the

ugly disgraces of civilization might be got rid of by the conscious will of intelligent persons; yet as I strove to stir people to this reform, I found that the causes of the vulgarities of civilization lay deeper than I had thought, and little by little I was driven to the conclusion that all of these uglinesses are but the outward expression of the innate moral baseness into which we are forced by our present form of Society, and that it is quite futile to attempt to deal with them from the outside.   Whatever I have written, or spoken on the platform on these social subjects, *is the result of the truths of Socialism meeting my earlier impulse*, and giving it a definite and more serious aim; and I can only hope . . . that any . . . who have found themselves hard-pressed by the sordidness of civilization, and have not known where to turn for encouragement, may receive the same enlightenment as I have.[16]

But this is anticipating the record of events.

As early as November, 1877, Morris made an interesting comment in a letter which discussed Matthew Arnold's lecture entitled *Equality*.   He felt himself to be at one with what Arnold there expressed, but held the opinion that if Arnold had any remedy for the then-existing social conditions, he was afraid to present it.   As for himself, he had already concluded that no rose-water could cure Society; the remedy for its ills must be far more heroic than that.   "Nothing can be done," he wrote, "till all men are made poor by common consent."[17]

Meantime Morris worked heart and soul for the cause expressed by the Eastern Question Association.   He

[16]Vallance, pp. 309-10.   The italics are mine,—A. A. von H.-P.
[17]Mackail, I, 366.

hoped great things, but he ended by becoming thoroughly disgusted with the Liberal party, to whose tenets he had always, though somewhat passively, it must be said, subscribed up to this time.   His disgust extended now to the inclusion of all politics.   On February 20, 1878, he wrote:

> Tomorrow I am going to Cambridge to give an address at the School of Art for Colvin.   As to my political career, I think it is at an end for the present; and has ended sufficiently disgustingly. After beating about the bush and trying to organize some rags of resistance to the war-party for a fortnight, after spending all one's time in committees and the like, I went to Gladstone with some of the workmen of Chesson, to talk about getting him to a meeting at the Agricultural Hall; he agreed, and was quite hot about it, and as brisk as a bee.   I went straight to the Hall, and took it for tomorrow: to work we fell, and everything got into train: but on Monday our Parliamentaries began to quake, and they have quaked the meeting out now.   The E. Q. A., was foremost in the flight, and really I must needs say they behaved ill in the matter.   Gladstone was quite ready to come up to the scratch and has behaved well throughout: but I am that ashamed that I can scarcely look people in the face, though I did my best to keep the thing up.   The working men are in a great rage about it, as they well may be: for I do verily believe we should have made it a success, though I don't doubt that there would have been a huge row.   There was a stormy meeting of the E. Q. A., yesterday, full of wretched little personalities, but I held my tongue—I am out of it now; I mean as to bothering my head about it; I shall give up reading the papers and shall stick to my work.[18]

For a time Morris kept his word.   He went back to his tapestry-weaving, carpet-making, dyeing, and to his lectures for the Society for the Protection of Ancient Buildings.   But not for long.   After his energetic mingling in the world of politics, and his intimate contact with social problems seen in a new light since his recent experiences, he could not feel himself entirely at his ease alone with his practice of the industrial arts and far away from the midst of things.   Henceforth Morris was never free from the shadow of the social problem.   To to the end of his life it followed him insistently.   In 1879 therefore Morris was back again in active politics. He joined the National Liberal League, an association

[18]Mackail, I, 361-62.

composed in a large part of the same men,—working-men Radicals,—who had been prominent in the Eastern Question Association. He made speeches at the meetings, and took a large part in the elections of 1880, which returned the Liberal Government to power. When he saw, however, that the social reform which he had been striving for "disappearing amid an ocean of Whiggery", weariness and disgust with the game political again overtook him.[19]

After his second disillusionment by politics Morris occupied himself for a short space in composing lectures on art. In 1878 he delivered before the Trades' Guild of Learning at Birmingham an address entitled *The Lesser Arts*. In August 1880, he wrote of his new activity:

By the way, I give my third lecture to the Trade Guild of Learning in October; that will be my autumn work, writing it, if I have any quiet time away from home. Also I have promised to lecture next March at the London Institute, subject *The Prospects of Architecture in Modern Civilization*. I will be as serious as I can over them, and when I have these last two done, I think of making a book on the subject, which still seems to me the most serious one that a man can think of; for 'tis no less than the chances of a calm, dignified, and therefore happy life for the mass of mankind.[20]

Although Morris busied himself as ever with the work of the firm of Morris & Company, with the Society for the Protection of Ancient Buildings, and with his new field as a lecturer on art, yet all of his letters at this time give indication in boldness of thought and vigor of language of the expanded outlook with which he viewed life. After his summer vacation in 1880 he wrote to Mrs. Burne-Jones: "You may imagine that coming back to this beastly congregation of smoke-dried swindlers and their slaves (whom one hopes one day to make their rebels) under the present circumstances does not make me much more in love with London, though I must admit to feeling this morning a touch of the 'all by oneself' independence which you wot of as a thing I like."[21]

[19]Mackail, II, 8.
[20]Mackail, II, 9-10.
[21]Mackail, II, 15.

Later in the autumn, when he was obliged to leave Kelmscott, he said:

I can't pretend not to feel being out of this house and its surroundings as a great loss. *I have more than ever at heart the importance for people of living in beautiful places. I mean the sort of beauty which would be attainable by all, if people could but begin to long for it. I do most earnestly desire that something more could be done than mere constant private grumbling and occasional public speaking to lift the standard of revolt against the sordidness which people are so stupid as to think necessary.*[22]

A more significant utterance of Morris's social doctrine is to be found in an address which he delivered in the autumn of 1881 at the annual meeting of the School of Science and Art connected with the Wedgewood Institute at Burslem. This address shows that his convictions on the problems of the day had deepened, and serves to explain a step he was soon to take.

I myself [Morris said in this lecture] am just fresh from an out-of-the-way part of the country near the end of the navigable Thames, where within a radius of five miles there are some half-dozen tiny village churches, every one of which is a beautiful work of art. These are the works of the Thames-side country bumpkins, as you would call them—nothing grander than that. If the same sort of people were to design and to build them now, they could not build anything better than the ordinary little plain Non-Conformist chapels that one sees scattered about new neighborhoods. That is what they correspond with, not an architect-designed Gothic church. The more you study architecture, the more certain you will become that I am right in this, and that what we have left us of earlier art was made by the unhelped people. Neither will you fail to see that it was made intelligently and with pleasure.

That last word brings me to a point so important that, at the risk of getting wearisome, I must add to it my old sentence and repeat the whole. Time was when everybody that made anything, made a work of art besides a useful piece of goods, *and it gave them pleasure to make it.* Whatever I doubt, I have no doubt of that.

I know that in those days life was often rough and evil enough, beset by violence, superstition, ignorance, slavery; yet sorely as poor folks needed a solace, they did not altogether lack one, and that solace was pleasure in their work. Much as the world has won since then, I do not think that it has won for all men such perfect happiness that we can afford to cast aside any solace that nature holds forth to us. Or must we forever be casting out one

[22]Mackail, II, 15-16. The italics are mine.

devil by another? Shall we never make a push to get rid of the whole pack of them at once?

As I sit at work at home, which is at Hammersmith, close to the river, I often hear some of that ruffianism go past the windows of which a good deal has been said in the papers of late, and has been said before at recurring intervals. As I hear the yells and shrieks and all the degradation cast on the glorious tongue of Shakespeare and Milton, as I see the brutal, reckless faces and figures go past me, it rouses the recklessness and brutality in me also, and fierce wrath takes possession of me, till I remember, as I hope I mostly do, that it was my good luck only of being born respectable and rich, that has put me on this side of the window among delightful books and lovely works of art, and not on the other side, in the empty street, the drink-steeped liquor shops, the foul and degraded lodgings. I know by my own feeling and desires what these men want, what would have saved them from this lowest depth of savagery; employment which would foster their self-respect and win the praise and sympathy of their fellows, and dwellings which they could come to with pleasure, surroundings which would soothe and elevate them: reasonable labor, reasonable rest. There is only one thing that can give them this—art. . . .

The work which is the result of division of labor, whatever else it can do, cannot produce art: which must, as long as the present system lasts be entirely confined to such works as are the work from beginning to end of one man—pictures, independent sculpture, and the like. As to these, on the one hand, they cannot fill the gap which the loss of popular art has made, nor can they, especially the more imaginative of them, receive the sympathy which should be their due. As things go, it is impossible for anyone who is not highly educated to understand the higher kinds of pictures. The aspect of this as regards people in general is to my mind much more important than that which has to do with the unlucky artist; but he also has some claim on our consideration; and I am sure that this lack of general sympathy of simple people weighs very heavily upon him, and makes his work feverish and dreamy, or crabbed and perverse.[23]

In a letter written on New Year's Day, 1881, full of serious thought on his own past life, and of the hopes now increasingly filling his mind, Morris said,

. . . my mind is very full of the great change which I hope is slowly coming over the world, and of which surely this new year will be one of the land-marks. Though to me, as I suppose to you, every day begins and ends a year, I was fain to catch hold of ancient

[23]This address has never been reprinted among the Morris lectures. It was published in one of the newspapers. Mr. Mackail quotes it almost in full. See II, 20 ff.

custom; nor perhaps will you think it ceremonious or superstitious if I try to join thoughts with you today in writing a word of hope for the new year, that it may do a good turn of work toward the abasement of the rich and the raising of the poor, which is of all things most to be longed for, till people can at last rub out of their dictionaries altogether these dreadful words rich and poor.[24]

A little latter Morris was driven to make the strongest utterance on social questions which he had thus far expressed.

I suppose [he wrote] you have seen about the sentence on Herr Most and read Coleridge's most dastardly speech to him: just think of the mixture of tyranny and hypocrisy with which the world is governed! These are the sort of things that make thinking people so sick at heart that they are driven from all interest in politics save revolutionary, which I must say seems like to be my case. Indeed, I have long known, or felt, say, that society in spite of its modern smoothness was founded on injustice and tyranny: but the hope in me has been that matters would mend gradually, till the last struggle, which must needs be mingled with violence and madness, would be so short as scarcely to count. But I must say matters like this and people's apathy about them shake one's faith in gradual progress.[25]

The same letter expressed Morris's pessimism concerning the success of the work done for the protection of ancient buildings. He felt that the foes against the Society— almost all educated as well as uneducated people—were too numerous. It was borne home to him that if people were to bestir themselves to save the beauty of the earth, as he often phrased it, they must have some love for that beauty; and he began to see also that only too few love the earth or its beauty, and that these few are so hopelessly in the minority that the triumphant majority will have its way until "all that is old is gone, and history has become a book from which the pictures have been torn". But despite his despondency—it was but the despondency of a moment—Morris kept on protesting, not only because it was his nature to protest, but because he had a little hope hidden away in a corner of his heart that something, some sort of culture would after all come of his unceasing efforts.

[24]Mackail, II, 24.
[25]Mackail, II, 24-25.

Morris wrote again a little later—and great indeed is
the contrast between these letters and those written
two or three years before in the social observation exhibited in them—

How people talk as if there were no wrongs of society against all
the poor devils it has driven demented in one way or another! Yet
I don't wonder at rich men trembling either: for it does seem as
though a rising impatience against the injustice of society was in
the air; and no wonder that the craziest heads, that feel this injustice most, breed schemes for setting it all right with a stroke of
lightning. . . . All political change seems to me useful now as
making it possible to get the social one: I don't mean to say that I
myself make any wide distinction between political and social; I
am only using the words in a common way.[26]

And in another letter of a week later he wrote:

I don't quite agree with you in condemning grumbling against
follies and ills that oppress the world at large, even among friends;
for you see it is but now and then that one has a chance of speaking
about the thing in public, and meantime one's heart is hot with it,
and some expression of it is like to quicken the flame even in those
that one loves and respects most, and it is good to feel the air laden
with the coming storm even as we go about our daily work or while
away time in light matters.   To do nothing but grumble and not to
act, that is throwing away one's life: but *I don't think that words on
our cause* that we have at heart *do nothing* but wound the air, even
when spoken among friends: 'tis at worst like the music to which
men go to battle.   Of course if the thing is done egotistically 'tis
bad so far; but that again, how to do it well or ill, is a matter of art
like other things.[27]

To do nothing but grumble and not to act was impossible for Morris. With his added vision of what civilization
had failed to accomplish, and what it ought to mean,
there was no possibility that he would retire altogether
to his tapestries or to his pottery; he was so constituted
and so trained that he must listen to the voice of the
unhappy and hearken to their pleading. So deep became his interest in this cause that even poetry seemed
to him to be "tommy-rot" compared with what he had
come to consider the realities of life. The expression
of an opinion akin to this is to be found in a letter which
touches on Swinburne's *Tristram of Lyonesse.*

[26]Mackail, II, 26.
[27]Mackail, II, 26-27.

I never could really sympathize with Swinburne's work; it always seemed to me to be founded on literature, not on nature. . . . Now time was when the poetry resulting merely from this intense study and love of literature might have been, if not the best, yet at any rate very worthy and enduring; but in these days when all the arts, even poetry, are likely to be overwhelmed under the mass of material riches which civilization has made and is making more and more hastily every day, riches which the world has made indeed, but cannot use to any good purpose; in these days the issue between art, that is, the godlike part of man, and mere bestiality, is so momentous, and the surroundings of life are so stern and unplayful, that nothing can take serious hold of people, or should do so, but that which is rooted deep in reality and is quite at first hand; there is no room for anything which is not forced out of a man of deep feeling because of its innate strength and vision.[28]

This letter also indicates that Morris had not yet conceived a definite hope such as he soon came to hold when he joined the Social Democratic Federation " . . . But in these days when all the arts including poetry, are like to be overwhelmed under the mass of material riches which civilization has made. . . . " are pessimistic words. The same note is found in another letter dated January 10, 1882:

Yet it seems to me as if my lot was a strange one; you see I work pretty hard, and on the whole pretty cheerfully, not altogether I hope, for mere pudding, still less for praise; and while I work I have the cause always in mind, and yet I know that the cause for which I specially work is doomed to fail, at least in seeming; I mean that art must go under, where or how ever it may come up again. I don't know if I explain what I am driving at, but it does sometimes seem to me a strange thing indeed that a man should be driven to work with energy and even with pleasure and enthusiasm at work which he knows will serve no end but amusing himself; am I doing nothing but make believe then, something like Louis XVI's lockmaking?[29]

And in still another letter the same tone recurs:

I hope I am not quite unhumble, or want to be the only person in the world untroubled; but I have been ever loth to think that there were no people going through life, not without pain indeed, but with simplicity and free from blinding entanglements. Such an one I want to be, and my faith is that it is possible for most men to be no worse. Yet indeed I am older, and the year evil; the sum-

[28]Mackail, II, 75.
[29]Mackail, II, 68.

merless season, and famine and war, and the folly of peoples come
back again, as it were, and the more and more obvious death of art
before it rises again, are heavy matters to a small creature like me,
who cannot choose but think about them, and can mend them
scarce a whit.[30]

The cause of art! This was the cause for which
Morris had worked through the specific arts, and for
which he, in this darkness before the dawn, had so little
immediate hope. But in these years of added understanding and widened vision, and in the lonely questioning
of himself as to why mankind for centuries had produced
nothing but sordid, aimless, ugly confusion, driven to
the conclusion that all civilization was to end in a
"counting-house on the top of a cinder heap", as he
himself expressed it, driven to the realization that the
cause of art was the cause of the people, he came to
think,—surely prompted by the spirit of the age, as well
as by his own heart,—that within the civilization he
found so odious and so beauty-less, the seeds of a great
change were already germinating. Socialism had come
to meet him, and he accepted it as the only solution of
how to make art again a part of daily life, how to make
men happy. For art to Morris was a broader thing
than most people deem it; to him it included all sound
work, and with it was bound up the problems of a sound
social life. Not by the road of Economics did William
Morris arrive at Socialism, but by the road of Art,—
not a by-path, as many unthinking people suppose,
finding in that solution of Morris's politics a potent reason
for despising his social ideals. Morris's whole theory
of art, of its province and of its production, as will be
shown later, takes into vital consideration the life of the
people and the economic conditions in which they work
and live. Ten years after Morris accepted Socialism,
he wrote:

When I took the step I was blankly ignorant of economics; I had
never so much as opened Adam Smith, or heard of Ricardo, or of
Karl Marx. Oddly enough I *had* read some of Mill, to wit, those
posthumous papers of his in which he attacks Socialism in Fourierist

[30]Mackail, II, 77.

guise.   In those papers he puts the arguments, as far as they go, clearly and honestly, and the result so far as I was concerned was to convince me that Socialism was a necessary change, and that it was possible to bring it about in our own days.   Those papers put the finishing touch to my conversion to Socialism.[31]

A few months after Morris had joined the Democratic Federation, he wrote to C. E. Maurice that he desired to convert all disinterested people of good will to what he called active and general Socialism.   The letter is further interesting to the student of Morris's social ideals and of the road by which he arrived at his faith.

I think that you, like myself, have really been a Socialist for a long time.   For my part, I used to think that one might further real Socialistic progress by doing what one could on the lines of ordinary middle-class Radicalism.   I have been driven of late into conclusions that I was mistaken; that Radicalism is on the wrong line, so to say, and will never develope into anything more than Radicalism; in fact, that it is made for and by the middle-classes and will always be under the control of rich capitalists: they will have no objection to its *political* development, if they can stop it there: but as to real social changes, they will not allow them if they can help it; you may see almost any day such phrases as this: "this is the proper way to stop the spread of Socialism" in the Liberal papers, the writer of the phrase never having taken the trouble to find out what Socialism meant, and also choosing to ignore the discontent, dumb indeed for the most part, which is widely spread even in England.   Meantime, I can see no use in people having political freedom unless they use it as an instrument for leading reasonable and manlike lives; no good in education if, when they are educated, people have slavish work to do, and have to live lives too beset with sordid anxiety for them to be able to think and feel with the more fortunate people who produce art and poetry and great thought.   This release from slavery, it is clear, cannot come to people so long as they are subjected to the bare subsistence wages which are a necessity of competitive commerce, and I cannot help thinking that the workmen will soon be finding out that for themselves.[32]

The hope which had come to Morris from the consciousness of a coming change, from the spirit of the age, kept him from being a mere grumbler, a mere pessimist; it kept him also from devoting his time and thought to the regeneration of art amid things as they were.   He

[31]Morris, *How I Became a Socialist*, pp. 9-10.
[32]Mackail, II, 103 ff.

had studied art and the conditions of its growth too thoroughly to be led into thinking that what is virtually dead can be raised to life merely by propping it up and regarding it as living. Death is a great change; to bring the dead again to life is a greater one, and requires quite different means.

PART II

THE
HISTORY OF MORRIS'S SOCIALISM

CHAPTER I

THE HISTORY OF MORRIS'S SOCIALISM

Art led William Morris to Socialism. This is the illuminating fact in connection with Morris's championship of Democracy. As a lover of Art, pondering on the art-poverty of the modern world, he found this art-poverty to have its roots in the unequal distribution of opportunity for men and women to express themselves artistically, or even to enjoy Art. Independently of socialistic thought Morris came to the conclusion that in Socialism lay the cure for the art-evils of modern industrialism.

Socialism in Morris's day was not new. The ethical principles of Socialism date back into antiquity; and indeed the reader may find a *Geschichte des antiken Kommunismus und Sozialismus* written by one Wilhelm Poehlmann. Then there is Plato's *Republic*, and Sir Thomas More's *Utopia*, Campanella's *City of the Sun*, Bacon's *New Atlantis*, Harrington's *Oceana*, and other like studies.[1] The Socialism, however, to which the art-loving Morris was to contribute his independently thought out protest against the evils of modern production had its birth in two modern phenomena. Socialism, as has been abundantly pointed out by others, professes to be the offspring of two Revolutions: that great upheaval which changed the center of industrial importance in England and dispelled the gloom and uncertainty caused by the dwindling of the English forests and by the water in its coal-mines,—the industrial Revolution; and that Revolution in thought which expressed itself so violently in France in 1789.[2] The

[1] See *Ideal Commonwealths*, Henry Morley, editor, New York, 1908; W. B. Guthrie, *Socialism before the French Revolution*, New York, 1907; Y. Guyot, *Sophismes socialistes et faits economiques*, Paris, 1907 (or Y. Guyot, *Socialistic Fallacies*, New York, 1910). This last book is of value for facts; but its reasonings and conclusions, for the most part, are not convincing to the well-informed and thinking student.

[2] Thomas Kirkup, *History of Socialism*.

The vagueness and the actual misconception which characterize many people's idea of the meaning of Socialism is due perhaps to the variety of definitions of the word. The following may be said to express a conception of Socialism prevalent

modern Socialist movement began in England with
Robert Owen; in France with Comte Henri de Saint-
Simon, both of whom were undoubtedly moved by the
spirit of liberty, equality, and fraternity, and both of
whom undoubtedly regarded labor as dignified and
worthy.   Robert Owen, a successful cotton manufacturer, had grown up in the midst of the Industrial
Revolution.   He knew from first-hand observation the
great abuses which characterized the new economic
régime; but more, he realized how wonderful might be
the services of technical and business advancement
especially if that advancement could be made the servant
of human well-being.   Accordingly he undertook the
task of making the new mechanism subservient to the
principle that it should aim at the welfare of all.   In
other words, he tried, by promoting protective labor
legislation and advancing his communistic theories, to
humanize the new industry.   Under the leadership of
Owen, then, early English Socialism arose as a protest
against the abuses and inequalities, the misery, the degradation, and the threatened moral and physical bank-
ruptcy of England that were emphasized by the Industrial
Revolution.   The student of economic history is familiar
with Owen's splendid social work at New Lanark, where
in 1800 at the age of twenty-nine he became manager
and part owner of a cotton mill, and also with his proposal before a committee of Parliament in 1817 that the
misery besetting Great Britain be abolished through
the organization of communistic settlements.[3]

in the United States: Socialism means democratic ownership, control, and use of
the land and capital employed in business of all kinds; public ownership of all
means of transportation and communication, and of all non-competitive business
enterprises; and ownership and control by the actual workers engaged therein of all
competitive business enterprises; with the added proviso that the use of land should
constitute the sole title to land.—*Socialist Platform*, in *International Socialist Review*, June, 1908, pp. 762-3.
        More briefly expressed, Socialism means democratic ownership, control, and
use of all land and capital employed in business.
        The word *socialism* appears to have been first used by Robert Owen in a private
conference in Philadelphia, on November 21, 1824.   In 1833 it was used in *The
Poor Man's Guardian.*   From England the words *socialism* and *socialistic* passed to
France.—Kirkup, pp. 3-4.
        [3]See Kirkup; also Frank Podmore; Robert Owen (biography) 2 vols.   For a
discussion of the failure of Owen's system, see Webb's *History of Trade Unionism.*
Although Owen's communistic enterprises failed and he lost prestige because of his

The first half of the nineteenth century was fruitful of social problems and social agitation. The Reform Bill of 1832 extended English suffrage, but it still left the laboring class without political power. Chartism arose to proclaim the workers' discontent and to emphasize "surplus value", of which the employer was declared to be defrauding the employee,—that value which represented the difference between what the worker was supposed to make, and what, according to the Iron Law of Wages, he received. Carlyle defined Chartism as bitter discontent grown fierce and mad.[4] But Chartism, as is well known, came to an unsuccessful end in 1848.

Stirred by the sufferings of the workers, Maurice, Kingsley, and Ludlow, in the years 1848-52 inaugurated the Christian Socialist movement against the evils of the competitive system and against the laissez-faire teaching of the Manchester School. Socialism rightly understood, the Christian Socialists maintained, was only Christianity applied to social reform. In the north of England this movement made itself of permanent value by joining with the Rochdale coöperative enterprise, which was started under the influence of Owenism in 1844, and has since grown to immense proportions.[5] The Christian Socialists aimed in general to make ethical and spiritual principles effective in industry and business, by substituting for the individual capitalists, self-governing bodies of profit-making workers.[6]

Owen's task in England had been to bend the new mechanism and the new industrialism to the service of humanity; in France St. Simon found before him a somewhat different problem. Although staggered by the French Revolution, continental feudalism still showed tenacious vitality. A new industrial world rest-

lax notions of marriage, Robert Owen will always be remembered with gratitude as the founder of infant schools in Great Britain, as the first manufacturer to shorten hours, as the energetic promoter of protective labor laws, as the inspiration of the Coöperative Movement, and as the exponent of the idea that the new industrialism should be for the benefit of humanity.

[4]Carlyle, *Past and Present*, p. 306.
[5]A convenient reference is C. R. Fay, *Co-operation at Home and Abroad*.
[6]Webb, *History of Trade Unionism*, pp. 207-8; Kirkup, pp. 71-2.

ing on hired labor had arisen, but the ancient, effete feudalism still held sway. St. Simon's desire and aim was to displace the parasitic rulers of obsolete feudalism by industrial chiefs and scientific leaders. These, instead of exploiting labor, were to control industrial France for the general good. Whereas, taught St. Simon, up to his times the law of humanity had been "the exploitation of man by man in the three stages of slavery, serfdom, and the proletariat, in the future the aim of human endeavor must be the exploitation of the globe by man associated to man." Another tenet of St. Simon's teaching was that the whole of society should strive to improve the moral and physical condition of the poorest class and should organize itself in the way that promised the most progress toward that end. Complete emancipation of woman and her full equality with man was included in St. Simon's program. In view of the free love ideas of some of the adherents of the school it should be emphasized that in its official declarations the school upheld the sanctity of the Christian marriage. A social hierarchy with position according to capacity, and reward according to service was also urged by this group. The movement gained much prominence in the Revolution of 1830 and soon set up a communistic settlement in Paris to practise its ideas. It was not long, however, before the extravagances of some of its adherents caused its dissolution.

St. Simon stood for the principle of authority, of centralization, for the idea of the State as the normal and dominant power; his contemporary, François Marie Charles Fourier, stood for the principle of local and industrial freedom. The dominant power, according to his ideas, should rest in the commune, or Phalange, as he named his proposed unit of social organization. The different Phalanges were to be joined in a world-wide union with a single elected head, resident at Constantinople. Labor in the Phalange was to be rewarded according to the talent; but hard and common work was to be paid most highly and pleasant work the least. Freedom, even to the extent of free love, and attractive and scientifically-conducted labor were to characterize the commune. A comfortable minimum share of the product of the Phalange was to go to each member. Of the balance five-twelfths was apportioned to labor, four-twelfths to capital, and three-twelfths to talent. Individual capital was to exist, and inequality of talent was not only to be recognized, but to be promoted and utilized. Fourier's Utopia could be no more than a Utopia because he underestimated the force of human egotism and because he advocated giving a free rein to human nature. His plan, however, embodies much valuable suggestion, especially in reference to the rights and the power in government of the local community.[7]

The theories of St. Simon and of Fourier appealed chiefly to the educated classes; but in France, as in England, the thirties inaugurated a distinctly working-class socialist movement. In England the Reform Bill of 1832, by enfranchising the upper middle class, had emphasized the abjectness of the artisan and the laborer. The Chartist agitation resulted. In France at Lyons, in 1831, the workers rose to arms with the device "Live working or die fighting".[8] Eight years later Louis Blanc's *Organization du travail* appeared in print and also Cabet's *Voyage en Icarie.* In 1840 Proudhon published his *Qu'est-ce-que la propriété?* Paris, particularly during the latter part of the reign of the bourgeois king, Louis Philippe (1830-48), became the seat of socialistic agitation. Among its visitors were Lasalle, founder of the German Social Democracy, Karl Marx, leader of the Scientific International Socialism, and Bakunin, the anarchist leader.

The schemes of St. Simon and of Fourier were largely imaginative and utopian; the working-class Socialism of Louis Blanc, however, connected itself with the course of French history. Blanc demanded as preparatory to social reorganization political democracy. The democratic state, he proposed, should when achieved, create industrial associations to which he would give the

[7]Kirkup, pp. 36-39.
[8]Kirkup, p. 42.

name of social workshops.   These workshops were gradually to supersede all private workshops.   The state was to furnish the necessary capital, draw up rules, and appoint officers for the first year; but when once started, a social workshop was to be a self-acting, self-supporting, and self-governing institution.   As a concession to less radical thought, Louis Blanc at first subscribed to the principle of remuneration according to capacity; but in 1848 he stood firmly upon the principle that exceptional endowments should find their reward in the development and opportunity for service to be found in the work to which they should be directed.   In France the European revolt of 1848 against obsolete political forms and in-stitutions and against irresponsible government resulted in universal male suffrage.   Blanc's social workshop plan was given a trial, but there is evidence that it was not given a fair test in the French National Workshops of 1848.   Thomas Kirkup declares that—"From the report of the Commission of Inquiry into the subject, subsequently instituted by the French government, and from the *History of the National Workshops*, written by their director, Émil Thomas, it is perfectly clear that the national workshops were simply a travesty of the proposals of Louis Blanc, established expressly to dis-credit them."   The private associations organized according to Blanc's plan were insufficiently subsidized by the government.   Besides, the months of stagnation and insecurity following the Revolution of February held out little prospect of success to any trade project.   It has been urged that the fair success of a few of the associations despite discouraging circumstances argues that Louis Blanc's plan had elements of vitality.   But Louis Blanc could not secure any solid success for his scheme.   He lacked both sufficient personal force and sufficient enduring political influence.   The Assembly, elected on the principle of universal male suffrage, meet-ing in May, found the French peasantry in disagreement with the working classes of the towns; the national work-shops were ordered closed; and the Paris insurrection of June yielded only a deluge of blood.[9]

[9]Kirkup, pp. 48-50.

Of the others thinking along the line of social reform it remains only to mention Pierre Joseph Proudhon. He regarded the duration of labor as the just measure of labor's reward. He would give as much to the poorest artisan as to the greatest artist; but he looked forward to a time when inequality of talent and of capacity would reach a minimum. He proposed a gradual reduction of interest, rent, and profits. For property he would eventually substitute individual possession with equal right to occupation. He is to be credited with realizing that the process of social transformation must be long and tedious.

The bloody days of June, 1848, gave French Socialism its quietus. The revolt removed or subdued the most enterprising leaders of the laboring class; and the prosperity of the Second Empire mitigated somewhat the evils and the abuses besetting the working classes.

In England the energy which might have gone into planning and working for Utopias was being directed to the development of trade unionism and to the movement for the extension of the franchise.[10]   Thomas Carlyle had not lifted up his voice in vain when, in his book on *Chartism*, he called upon the upper classes to come to a clear and genuine understanding of the intrinsic meaning of the lower classes, and to seek a clear interpretation of the thought which was tormenting the wild, inarticulate souls of the workers.   Carlyle felt sure that an understanding of the working class problem would mean its solution, for "no man at heart means injustice".   In this connection it may be recalled that Robert Owen was an employer and that with the aid of certain other high-minded manufacturers, he organized the Society for National Regeneration, the most definite proposal of which was the Eight Hour day. This Society brought about the Short Time Committees in the textile towns. The Eight Hour day did not succeed, but the persistent agitation of these committees resulted in the Ten Hour law. Carlyle further preached the necessity of translating statistics into really human terms, by which he

[10]Sidney Webb, *Socialism in England*, pp. 18-19.

meant specifically that the wages which a worker gets and the bread that he buys with his wages are not all of life. His eloquent and satirical words on the laissez-faire policy and his excellent analysis of injustice did not go unheeded, although they made less impression than they deserved.[11] Men indeed like Maurice and Kingsley were stirred to action. Ruskin adopted Carlyle's work-gospel and called him Master.[12] Even today the powerful eloquence of his voice is not without its potency.

Ruskin's first utterances, however, were directed against the vulgar utilitarianism, the corrupt and over-pampered civilization, and the mechanical conception of progress which marked the age, rather than to the Condition of England question.[13] It was entirely natural, therefore, that he should soon become interested in various schemes for working-class education. In 1857 his lectures on the *Political Economy of Art* denounced the evil effects of competition and set forth the doctrine that the State ought to educate and organize the artistic ability of the nation. It was not long after this that he attacked the assumptions of current political economy and assailed the modern industrial system for its waste, its injustice, and its inhumanity.[14] Comte, John Stuart Mill, Darwin, and Spencer reinforced the teachings of Carlyle and of Ruskin, while direct application to the workers of these various philosophic protests was made by Marx and Lasalle. With all of these eloquent voices rising against things as they were, with the conception of a Social Organism taking hold of the minds of the people, the fatted peace of the English bourgeoisie could not but be disturbed. Industrial development likewise forced upon the State the necessity of doing something to protect the masses against exploitation by capital with the result that Parliamentary acts for their protection were slowly wrung from the law-makers.[15]

---

[11]Carlyle, *Chartism*, pp. 309 ff. See also *Past and Present*.
[12]Collingwood, *Life and Work of Ruskin*, I, 137-38; Ruskin, *Praeterita*, p. 250; *On the Old Road*, I, 276; *Political Economy of Art, or A Joy Forever*.
[13]Ruskin, *Modern Painters*, II, 3.
[14]Ruskin, *Unto This Last*, and *Munera Pulveris*.
[15]S. Webb, *Socialism in England*, pp. 19-20.

To the ferment already rising to the surface the socialistic ideas of Lasalle and Marx contributed not a little.
Other contemporary chiefs of German Socialism were
Friederich Engels and Rodbertus.   But of this group
Ferdinand Lasalle was the first to make his impress on
history as the originator of the Social Democratic movement in Germany.   Lasalle's social work began in 1862
when he gave a lecture on *The Workingmen's Programme*,
in which he tried to show that a new historical period
was dawning in which the interests of labor would be
paramount.   In his *Open Letter* in 1863, sometimes called
the Charter of German Liberalism, Lasalle advocated
an independent political party to be made up of working men.   He declared that the coöperative schemes of
the Progressist party were inadequate, and he argued
that, under existing conditions, the Iron Law of Wages
prevented improvement.   He advocated productive
associations to be established by the State.   These
should rest upon universal suffrage and should secure
to the workers the full product of their labor.   The same
year, 1863, he launched at Leipsic the Universal Workingmen's Association.   Lasalle's schemes were not
carried into practice, whereas the coöperative plans of
the Progressist Party became a huge practical success;
yet when Lasalle fell in a duel in 1864, Prussia lost a
social leader who had done efficient pioneer work for
German Social Democracy.[16]

While Lasalle was a mere boy of eleven, a number of
German exiles formed in Paris in 1836 a secret society
under the name of the League of the Just, the principles
of which were communistic.   Becoming involved in an
uprising in Paris in 1839, the group fled to London, where
the League, falling under the influence of Karl Marx in
1847 reorganized, taking the name "Communist League".
The old motto of the League, "All men are brethren"
was replaced by a new battle-cry, "Proletarians of all
lands unite".   Seventeen years later this battle-cry re-
sounded through the world as the watch-word of the
International Working Men's Association.   The Com-

[16]Kirkup, pp. 73-122.

munist League was too young and too weak to be very effective in the Revolution of 1848; the reactionaries were victorious, and besides, a period of considerable industrial prosperity followed. Marx withdrew to his London study, and the first attempt at an international combination of workers came to an end in 1852.   The people, however, continued to be restive. At the London International Exhibition, which was attended by a deputation of French workmen, the beginning of another International showed itself.   The next year, 1863, a French deputation went to England, and in 1864 the International Association of Working Men was organized to promote the protection, the progress, and the complete emancipation of the laboring class.   Marx was the moving spirit of this organization.   His leadership was all the more earnest because he was firm in the belief that (1) although there had been an enormous development in industry and in wealth since 1848, the misery of the masses had not diminished; (2) the successful struggle for a Ten Hour day meant the breaking down of the political economy of the middle classes; and (3) that the productive association of a few daring "hands" had proved that industry on a large scale could be carried on without capitalist masters.[17]   It was the aim of the International to unite all workers for a realization of Socialism.[18]   It is of interest that at the first congress of the International, socialistic principles were declared only in a general way; the emphasis was placed upon a gradual reduction of work to eight hours, and upon a very comprehensive plan for the intellectual and technical education of the working classes.   At the second congress at Lausanne in 1867 it was resolved that means of transportation and communication should become State property.   Encouragement was offered to Coöperative associations and to organizations to raise wages; but the besetting strife of socialistic bodies between doctrinairism and opportunism raised its head

[17]In 1847 the British Parliament passed a ten hour law for women and young persons.—Bulletin U. S. Bureau of Labor, 70:548.   See also Hutchins and Harrison, *History of the Factory Acts*, and also Kirkup, p. 180.
[18]Rae, *Contemporary Socialism*, pp. 151-2.

in the fear expressed that such associations and organizations might become compatible with the capitalistic system. The third congress, which convened at Brussels in 1868, was more outspokenly socialistic than its two predecessors. This congress declared that not only agencies of transportation and communication, but also mines, forests, and land should become the common property of a democratic State, and should be handed over by the State to associations of workers who would use them under rational and equitable rules to be determined by society. Coöperative and mutual credit associations were endorsed as the only means whereby the workers could gain control of capital. This third congress also proposed a better method of organizing strikes and urged shorter hours of labor as an indispensable condition to securing a thorough system of scientific, professional, and industrial instruction. Declaration was made that "Labor must have its full right and entire reward", and a universal strike was recommended in case the impending war between France and Germany should break out. The Congress of 1869 was without special significance except for a vote against the abolition of inheritance.[19]

The International repeatedly gave substantial help to the English trade unionists by preventing cheap continental labor from going to England, and by winning substantial success in support of the Paris bronze workers, locked out in 1867. It was declared in 1870 that 800,000 American workers had adopted its principles, and it soon had affiliations in every country in Western Europe. It was handicapped, however, by the necessary looseness of its organization, and by the insignificance of its financial resources; and besides, it was said that many of the affiliated unions were in the International for what they could get out of it, rather than for what they could give to the movement. The English trade unionists, intent on more practical problems at home, never took a deep interest in the International. The Socialists of Germany were disunited, poor, and much hampered

[19]Kirkup, pp. 183-6.

by the police. In addition to the latent strife between doctrinairism and opportunism, Bakunin and his following of anarchists, who joined in 1868, brought in an element of discord. At the instance of Marx the anarchists were expelled by the Hague congress of 1869. At this time also the headquarters of the general council, the governing body, were removed to New York. The end of the International was in sight. Another congress was held in Geneva in 1873, and then followed its quiet dissolution. The International had failed of permanency; nevertheless it had done a good service for humanity by emphasizing the common interest that all countries have in the welfare of the laboring class. Furthermore, it broke the way for future International congresses,[20] and perhaps it may be said that it had an influence leading to the organization at the Paris Exposition in 1900 of the International Association of Labor Legislation, which aims at the protection of the worker against exploitation; and hence at the promotion of human welfare, especially through uniform labor legislation. After the fall of the International some hopes were entertained of starting a socialist movement in the larger cities of England, but they came to nothing. Foreign refugees had a small club in London which attracted to it some few of the workingmen; but beyond that, the English proletariat attempted to exert no influence for several years.

In 1880, however, the English working class movement was startled out of its "complacent quietism" by Henry George's *Progress and Poverty*. This book immediately attained a great popularity throughout England; and although apparently every hope of a new organization of society had died when the International fell to pieces in 1873, this book galvanized them all into palpitating life. Converts of Henry George's views formed themselves into little clubs, many of which soon became actively socialistic.[21]

[20]Kirkup, pp. 186-89, 193-6.
[21]S. Webb, *Socialism in England*, p. 21; Sidney and Beatrice Webb, *History of Trade Unionism*, p. 361.

Mention has already been made of the fact that Morris's enthusiasm for politics cooled after the elections of 1880, which returned the Liberals to power, when he realized what this party was doing with its power, and how little it really cared for the reforms which appeared to be of the greatest importance to the more earnest members of his party. The measures taken in 1881 by Gladstone's ministry against the Irish Land League disgusted still more of the conscientious Radicals; and besides the aggressive Eastern policy of the party which they had put into power, was more than they could endure. Promised fiscal reforms, reforms of the Land Tax, the Tea Tax, and others as pressing slipped from the memory of this Liberal "party of progress". Under such circumstances it was not strange that those who had these reforms really at heart should form a club of their own. In March, 1881, these English insurgents organized themselves into a body called the Democratic Federation to promote measures of Radical reform under the leadership of H. M. Hyndman, Herbert Burrows, Miss Helen Taylor, Joseph Cowan, and others. The only distinctively Socialist article in their first program was for the nationalization of the land, though there can be no doubt that the club was socialistic in its temper and aims, and became increasingly so as time went on.[22] In 1883 the Federation definitely adopted the socialistic principles of Karl Marx and a little later changed its title to the Social Democratic Federation. G. Bernard Shaw in his Fabian Essay on the *Transition to Social Democracy*, comments interestingly on this movement:

Numbers of young men, pupils of Mill, Spencer, Comte, and Darwin, roused by Mr. Henry George's *Progress and Poverty*, left aside evolution and free thought; took to insurrectionary economics; studied Karl Marx; and were so convinced that Socialism had only to be put clearly before the working-classes to concentrate the power of their immense numbers in one irresistible organization, that the Revolution was fixed for 1889—the anniversary of the French Revolution—at latest. I remember being asked satirically and publicly at that time how long I thought it would take to get Socialism into working order if I had my way. I replied with

[22]Webb, *Socialism in England*, pp. 22-23.

a spirited modesty that a fortnight would be ample for the purpose. When I add that I was frequently complimented on being one of the more reasonable Socialists, you will be able to appreciate the fervor of our conviction, and the extravagant levity of our practical ideas.[23]

Even before the Democratic Federation openly and definitely became socialistic, Morris had been drawn into touch with it by his previous association with London Radicals and working-class leaders. He had known H. M. Hyndman since 1879 as well as others who held the same beliefs.[24] In October 1882 he sold a large part of his valuable library containing early printed books and sagas from Iceland to help on the cause of Socialism, an act of devotion needing no comment. On the thirteenth of January 1883, on the very day on which he was unanimously elected Honorary Fellow of Exeter College, Oxford, he joined the Democratic Federation. That he fully realized the import of the step which he was taking is shown by his own words: "I am truly glad that I have joined the only society I could find which is definitely socialistic."[25] It was a characteristic act. Now that he had conceived a hope of realizing his social ideal, Morris could not feel as he did for the cause of art, for the cause of the people, and remain inactive. His idea of what one should do when one clearly sees his duty repudiated such a course. In a lecture delivered in 1884 occur these words:

The cause of art is the cause of the people. We well-to-do people, those of us who love art, not as a toy, but as a thing necessary to the life of man, have for our best work the raising of the standard of life among the people. How can we of the middle classes, we the capitalists, and the hangers-on, help? By renouncing our class, and on all occasions when antagonism rises up between the classes, casting in our lot with the victims; those who are condemned at the best to lack of education, refinement, leisure, pleasure, and renown; and at the worst, to a life lower than that of the most brutal of savages. There is no other way.[26]

[23]*Fabian Essays in Socialism*, edited by G. Bernard Shaw, p. 230.
[24]Vallance, p. 315.
[25]Mackail, II, 86-87.
[26]Mackail, II, 84-85; cf. the view of St. Simon, p. 74.

That there was no other way for one who had come to believe as he did, Morris held consistently to the end. And for a man of his position and prominence there was plenty of protesting from friends and admirers. It is his glory what when he saw a duty so large as that of renouncing his own class, he did it resolutely and with joy. The philosopher who evolves a "system" is not alone in his service to the world. The person who inspires or who leads, who lives a philosophy consistently, though perhaps no ordered body of foggy metaphysics makes his name a wonder to the gaping earth, may accomplish an amount almost immeasurable for the betterment of the world.

The elation of the Democratic Federation over Morris's membership in it can well be imagined. Already his was a famous name both in poetry and in art. H. M. Hyndman testifies to the value of capable recruits to the new cause. Among their number they had some very able men, but Morris, with his great reputation and high character doubled their strength.[27] Mr. Hyndman also bears witness to the enthusiasm of the new member. "He was as ready to do anything as the youngest and least known among us. In fact, he resented attempts being made to keep him back from doing things which really he ought not to have done. Writing, speaking, in and out of doors, conferring, full of zeal and brimming over with good humor and suggestion."

Morris was indeed a willing disciple. He set to work industriously to understand the economic side of Socialism, and "even tackled Marx," he wrote, "though I must confess that, whereas I thoroughly enjoyed the historical part of *Capital*, I suffered agonies of confusion of brain over reading the pure economics of that great work."[28]   His constant association with Mr. Hyndman, Belfort Bax, Scheu, and others, and his participation in the many propagandist meetings held continually by

[27]*Justice*, October 6, 1896. Also reprinted in the pamphlet, *How I Became a Socialist*, by Morris, p. 7. See also H. M. Hyndman, *The Record of an Adventurous Life*, pp. 320-21.
[28]Morris, *How I Became a Socialist*, p. 7.

the Federation, filled in the gaps in his knowledge of the scientific aspect of Socialism.   But he found the task more difficult than he at first supposed it would be, for he wrote to Mrs. Burne-Jones: "I naturally find it harder work to understand the subject of Socialism in detail now I am along side it, and often get beaten in argument when I know all the same I am really in the right, but but of course this only means more study."[29]

The work for the new cause took an ever-increasing amount of time and energy from Morris's business and from his writing.   Lovers of Morris's poetry deplore his departure from the realm of poetry and art to that of social reform; and when they feel obliged to refer to this part of his life, they condescendingly call his conversion to the new faith (for they wrongly deem it a conversion), a weakness to which he succumbed out of the generosity and enthusiasm of his poetic nature,—a vagary of the artistic temperament, as it were,—and therefore pardonable in so great a man.   They also consider, in complete ignorance of the facts of the case, that he saw the error of his ways about 1890 and returned once more, like a sort of prodigal son, to the respectable class of his fathers.   What Morris himself thought of poetry compared with work for the cause of men may be seen in a letter which he wrote August 21, 1883, to Mrs. Burne-Jones, who had made an effort to bring him back to the creation of poetry:

I am touched by your kind anxiety about my poetry; but you see, my dear, there is first of all my anxiety, which I am bound to confess has made a sad coward of me; and then, though I admit I am a conceited man, yet I really don't think anything I have done (when I consider it as I should another man's work) of any value except to myself; except as showing my sympathy with history and the like.   Poetry goes with the hand-arts, I think, and like them has now become unreal; the arts have got to die, what is left of them, before they can be born again.   You know my views on the matter; I apply them to myself as well as to others.   This would not, I admit, prevent my writing poetry any more than it prevents my doing my pattern work, because the mere personal pleasure of it urges one to the work; but it prevents my looking at it as a sacred duty, and the grief aforesaid is too strong and dis-

[29]Mackail, II, 112.

quieting to be overcome by a mere inclination to do what I *know* is unimportant work.   Meantime the propaganda gives me work to do, which, unimportant as it seems, is part of a great whole which cannot be lost, and that ought to be enough for me.[30]

By April, Morris was lecturing steadily and regularly for the Federation, and was becoming more and more positive in his tone and utterance.   A month later he was put on the executive board of the Social Democratic Federation.   This meant more work for him as well as contributing more money; for Morris was liberal both with energy and money in assisting the cause of Socialism.

In the autumn of 1883 he began to worry about the dissension which he found within the Federation.   He thought, and others also, that some of the members were too sanguine of speedy change, too anxious to form quickly a Socialist party.   To Morris this policy meant compromise, and the carrying along with them of people who only agreed with them in a few particulars, and were by no means ready to accept the Socialist program.   He was of the opinion that the Federation should welcome only real converts,—those who would presumably always remain faithful to the cause.   At the same time, he felt a trifle downcast because the workingmen did not,— and he soon saw that it could not be hoped that they would,—support constructive Socialism immediately.   He saw readily that their great need was strong leaders from the working-classes, men who would be content to remain working-class leaders. Morris had to struggle also against the misunderstandings which people had of the principles of the Federation; he found then, as others find to-day, that even well-educated and well-read people confuse Socialism and Anarchism.[31]   But in spite of his feeling of dissatisfaction over the differences of method in the Federation, he nevertheless signed the Manifesto when it came out in June.   He could not agree entirely with its wording; yet his signature testified to his general accordance with its substance.   Events soon showed, however, that his acceptance of it had not been final.

[30]Mackail, II, 109-10.
[31]Mackail, II, 110-11.

So permeated had Morris's thought become with the social ideal to the attainment of which he was now actively bending all of his forces, that he found it impossible to lecture on Art and its principles without leavening the whole with his Socialist doctrine. Even his letters of this period were dominated by his new faith. Conservatives and those who had a conventional knowledge of art were willing and eager to hear him lecture on the theory of art, but they were indignant or mystified when he told them that in order to have a real, popular art, the basis of society must be changed, and frankly appealed to him for assistance in bringing about the new order of things. As early as October, 1883, when he was asked to lecture in Manchester to the Ancoats Brotherhood, he replied that he had only one subject upon which to talk: namely, the Relation of Art to Labor. At the same time he took advantage of the opportunity to announce to them openly that he was a Socialist, and that all that he would say would be colored by the doctrine which he had accepted.[32] Even when he was invited to go to Oxford to address the Russell Club, an organization holding somewhat advanced ideas on social questions, but not definitely socialistic, he informed his audience at the end of his lecture that he spoke only as the agent of the Democratic Federation, and as such, he called upon them to join his organization. Oxford was horrified, but Morris, it must be said, could not be blamed. He fully explained beforehand that he was a Socialist and that he would speak as one. Apparently Oxford was unable to believe that a man in Morris's position, an artist, a poet, a man of wealth at the head of an art firm could really be a Socialist like H. M. Hyndman and other Socialist agitators, whom they felt thoroughly must certainly be considered outside of the pale of respectability.

Naturally enough Morris received from various sources many anxious inquiries concerning his beliefs during his first year of declared Socialism; and many were the letters which he was obliged to write in explanation and

[32]Mackail, II, 114.

even defense of his actions. To Mrs. Burne-Jones, who suggested that education to her mind was the one thing needful before any successful attempt could be made to change the present system of society, he replied:

Every one who has thought over the matter must feel your dilemma about education; but think of the many not uneducated people that you know and you will I am sure see that education will not cure people of the grossest social selfishness and tyranny, unless socialistic principles form part of it. Meantime I am sure it is right, whatever the apparent consequences may be, to stir up the lower classes, (damn the word) to demand a higher standard of life for themselves,[33] not merely for themselves or for the sake of the material comfort it will bring, but for the good of the whole world and the regeneration of the conscience of man: and this stirring up is part of the necessary education which must in good truth go before the reconstruction of society: but I repeat that without laying before the people this reconstruction, our education will but breed tyrants and cowards, big, little, and least, down to the smallest who can screw out money from standing by to see another man working for him.

The one thing I want you to be clear about is that I *cannot help* acting in the matter, and associating myself with anybody that has the root of the matter; and you know, and it may ease your kind heart respecting me, that those who are in the thick of it, and trying to do something, are not likely to feel so much of the hope deferred which hangs about the cause as onlookers do.[34]

To Mr. Horsfall he said that while he agreed that the rich do not act as they do from malice, yet their position forces them to keep the workers in ignorance both of their right and of their power. His correspondent had evidently expressed the opinion that individuals of good will, of any class, if only of sufficient numbers and zealous enough, could bring about the desired change. To this Morris replied that for his part he thought the basis of all change must be, as it had ever been, the antagonism of the classes, and that though a few upper or middleclassmen might work hard for the proletariat, from the very nature of the case, the higher classes of society

[33]In holding to this thought of educating the workers to demand a higher standard of living for themselves Morris is at one with many a friend of humanity who could not be called a Socialist.

[34]Mackail, II, 112-13. See also a letter to Mr. Horsfall written in 1883: "I have long felt sure that commercialism must be attacked at the root before we can be on the road for those improvements of life which you and I so much desire ...."

must resist the abolition of class distinction. Further-more, Morris thought that amelioration of the lot of the poor would not do much permanent good, except that the poor would gradually get more power and be therefore better able both to voice and otherwise to show their dis-content, for starvelings cannot bring about a revolution.[35] Capital has created the proletariat, he wrote, and in the proletariat must lie the salvation.   It will, and indeed it cannot help but destroy capital, for evolutionary forces are on its side.

Up to the end of 1883 the Democratic Federation, which about this time modified its title to Social Dem-ocratic Federation, had had no press through which to give notices of lectures and other necessary announce-ments, or to disseminate its ideas.   Early in 1884 Edward Carpenter provided the needed funds for starting a journal, significantly named *Justice*.   The first issue appeared on January 19, 1884; and thereafter Morris not only generously paid the weekly deficit, but also contributed numerous articles until December 20th of the same year.   Among his articles were three of his *Chants for Socialists*.[36]   The May and June numbers contained two articles written by him, entitled *A Factory as it Might Be*, and *Work in a Factory as it Might Be*.[37]

The whole of the year 1884 Morris gave up to lecturing in and out of London.   He visited Manchester, Leeds, Sheffield, Glasgow, and many smaller places, organizing branches of the Democratic Federation wherever possi-ble.   He had four addresses which he was prepared to give on the subject of Socialism: *Useful Work versus Useless Toil; Art and Labor; Misery and the Way Out;* and *How We Live and How We Might Live*.[38]

[35]Here is a suggestion of opportunist Socialism, such as differs in ultimate but not in the immediate aim from the ideas and purposes of the social reformer as distinguished from the Socialist.
[36]The first of the *Chants for Socialists* appeared in September, 1883.   It is en-titled *The Day is Coming*, and is included in the little volume, *Poems by the Way*, pp. 107-112.
[37]Vallance, p. 321.
[38]The first and fourth of these lectures appeared later in *Signs of Change*, a col-lection of seven lectures on Socialism, published in 1888.

It is interesting to note at this point that William Morris accepted so completely the doctrines of Socialism that he forgot altogether the forces of evolution. His own enthusiastic utterances and assiduity in the work of propaganda led him to believe that the ideals of social justice for which he was laboring were immediately practicable. All that was necessary, he thought, was that people should understand his doctrine. To understand with him was to act. So it must be with all others. If only people could be made to see and carry out the program, happiness for the unhappy was surely within grasp. A long, weary road of disappointment and seeming failure lay ahead of him before he learned that evolutionary forces must have their way and must work in their own good time. That human nature must be reckoned with was brought home to him again and again in his own small group of idealists who all had different ways and means for carrying out the program of social reform.

Mention has already been made of the dissension within the Social Democratic Federation. Morris had already on more than one occasion been obliged to play the part of the peacemaker. There came a time, however, when his distrust of certain members became so strong that he concluded that he must become a leader of a party within a party.[39] He and a little circle of followers still held to the fundamental principles enunciated by the Federation, but there had arisen the usual differences of opinion among the members as to the advisability of mixing in current politics, and also a difference as to methods of spreading their doctrines.[40] Morris and his party believed firmly enough in the socialist principle of public control over the instruments of wealth production, but they believed also that this control should be exercised by free communal groups. They feared an over-centralized administration. In addition Morris had an overpowering dislike of the methods of contemporary politics, and was consequently

[39]Mackail, II, 126.
[40]Rae, p. 85.

strongly opposed to their use. "What a spectacle of shuffling, lies, vacillation, and imbecility does the Game Political offer us! If we ally ourselves to any of the present parties they will use us as a catspaw; and on the other hand, if a Socialist candidate slips through into Parliament, he will only do so at the expense of his principles."[41] Morris preferred to confine the activity of the Socialists to the work of educating the masses in the principles and ideals of his party. Political agitation and Parliamentary action on the part of the Federation meant certain failure to him. Besides, he feared the sort of government Mr. Hyndman and his associates wished to establish,—a species of State Socialism in which he saw colossal opportunity for tyranny.[42] With so strong a distrust of the spirit and policies leading in the Social Democratic Federation Morris decided to have nothing more to do with it.

The occasion of the break was a petty occurrence which can be of little concern to any one after this lapse of time; the break, however, was inevitable owing to the deeper differences explained above.[43] On December

[41]Webb, *Socialism in England*, pp. 33-34.

[42]Vallance, p. 328.

[43]In a letter written to a Mr. Robert Thomsen, who made inquiries of Morris about Socialism, Morris wrote the following concerning his secession from the Social Democratic Federation:

"The whole thing really lies in this statement: the attempt to establish absolutism led to its usual results and had to be backed by the usual means . . . I plainly expressed my opinion as to Hyndman's absolutism and self-seeking. . . . To my mind, Hyndman's tendencies have led the Social Democratic Federation or at least were leading it into a futile and even dangerous policy, nor could I in any case have worked with him long in carrying out that policy. It has meant adventure, show, and advertisement, which would have found us out in the long run, and shown us to be a small party without organization and with no very clear aims. Hence all these theatrical boasts and warnings about immediate revolution, which frightened those who were ignorant of our condition away from us, and disgusted those who know how weak we are, many of whom are just the men who would be the staunchest if occasion offered. Hence also the perpetual sneers at, and abuse of the radicals, who, deluded as we must think them, are after all the men from whom our recruits must come. Hence attacks on foreigners as foreigners, or at least sneers at them; coquetting also with jingoism in various forms, all of which mean waiting about to see what can be made of the political situation, if perhaps at the best one may attain to a sort of Bismarckian State Socialism, or as near as we can get to it in England. I cannot stand all this: it is not what I mean by Socialism either in aim or in means: I want a real revolution, a real change in society: society, a great organic mass of well-regulated forces used for bringing about a happy life for all. And the means for attaining it are simple enough; education in Socialism, and organization for the time when the crisis shall force action upon us: nothing else will

30, 1884, Morris rented new quarters, and he and the other seceders formed the Socialist League.[44] Morris was elected the treasurer of the new organization and the editor of the journal, the *Commonweal*, founded at the same time. The *Commonweal* made its first appearance in February, 1885. In his first editorial Morris wrote courageously,—using the language which the socialistic propaganda has made familiar: "It is our duty to attack unsparingly the miserable system which would make all civilization end in a society of rich and poor, of slaves and slave-owners. . . . We assume as a matter of course, that a government of privileged persons, hereditary and commercial, cannot act usefully toward the community; their position forbids it; their arrangements

do us any good at present: the revolution cannot be a mechanical one, though the last act of it may be civil war, or it will end in reaction after all.

"Nothing hinders us from this education and organizing work: if there are laws against it, we know nobody will dare to put them in force: why then should we swagger about violence which we know we cannot use: when the time comes to use it, we shall not need to tell everybody beforehand.

"I finish by saying that whatever faults I have, I am by no means a quarrelsome man; and if I could have avoided this quarrel I would have done so. In fact, I have gone on hoping against hope for the last six months that the differences might heal up: but the truth is that Hyndman is determined to be master, and will not accept any other place, and he cannot change his nature and be otherwise than a jingo and a politician if he tries. I can only hope that some of his friends may keep him straight for awhile; but I believe that in time they will be driven to the same conclusion as we have been—that they cannot work with him.

"As you may have heard, we have formed another body, the Socialist League, from which you will shortly hear; I can only say of it that it begins at all events with the distinct aim of making Socialists by educating them, and of organizing them to deal with politics in the end; that it expects single-heartedness from its members and fraternal co-operation, and that it will not suffer any absolutism amongst it. . . . "

In another letter to the same gentleman Morris wrote: " . . . I must say that the latter part of your letter in which you point out a real difference of opinion amongst the S. D. F. explains why we did not hesitate to resign when we saw how far the split had gone: I mean that quite apart from any personal differences we saw the difference of opinion which was sure to widen. Now a propagandist body cannot afford to have two parties in it; however they may be personally, they had much better work apart, otherwise we shall only have an image of the parliament with its ceaseless wrangles and no work done. Understand that I no longer fear differences of opinion in our ranks: only when the difference is established, let us separate and work side by side rather than wrangle on together: thus we shall keep friends and the cause will be sped. Of course this doesn't suit the tactics of the political adventure which wants to get together a political party for immediate political ends, and they will call these views anarchical: I say they are common-sense, as applied to a weak party with no means of action and with the one necessary aim of building up opinion."—Elbert Hubbard, *William Morris Book*, pp. 52-57. See also H. M. Hyndman, *The Record of an Adventurous Life*, p. 328., for Mr. Hyndman's account of the break.

[44]Mackail, II, 129-132.

for the distribution of the plunder of the workers, their struggles for the national share of the exploitation of barbarous peoples are nothing to us, except so far as they may give us an opportunity of instilling Socialism into men's minds."[45]

The organization of the Socialist League brought Morris even greater notoriety than had his connection with the Social Democratic Federation.   He was openly sneered at and called the poet-upholsterer and a hypocrite because he preached Socialism and was, at the same time, a capitalist.   This is a criticism which is still heard of Morris and still seriously discussed.   In his own day he was often asked to justify publicly his position as the head of a manufacturing firm and an employer of labor.   He admitted that his position seemed to be a false one, but he invariably replied that under the existing system and organization of society it was impossible to give up his position as a capitalist and take his place among the workers.   He declared himself ready to relinquish that position when the State was ready to take over his business and to manage it socially.   Until that time, to give up his capital would be to hand it over to another capitalist who would be compelled by the status quo to exploit labor.[46]   He maintained that all capitalists were but minute links in the immense chain of the tremendous organization of competitive commerce, and that only the complete unriveting of that chain would really free him with the others.   "It is this very sense of the helplessness of our individual efforts," he wrote, "which arms us against our class, which compels us to take an active part in an agitation which, if it be successful, will deprive us of our capitalist position."[47] In June, 1884, Morris drew up a memorandum of the whole matter, going with considerable detail into the figures.   In his business, he and five others shared directly in the profits.   Two other workers received a bonus on the goods produced by them; and the others

[45]*Commonweal*, February, 1885.
[46]Vallance, p. 320.
[47]Mackail, II, 134.

of the staff were paid fixed wages,—by the piece, by the day, or by the hour.   Two or three people who were of no use to the business were kept on the live-and-let-live principle.   All of the workers received a higher wage than was usual in their trades.   According to his survey of the situation, Morris concluded that if he gave up his own share of the profits, which included his own salary as the manager, designer, and workman, and also the interest on £15,000 capital invested, and took instead the wages of a highly skilled workman of £200 a year, the sum of only £16 could be given each workman in addition to the wages paid.   He believed that nothing permanent would be gained by this arrangement, because although the small number of working men whom he benefitted directly would undoubtedly be better off, yet the result would be that they would probably save their money and become capitalists in their turn.   He was willing, he maintained, to see workmen escape from their positions as wage-slaves; yet he did not wish to be responsible for increasing the number of the capitalist class.   From the socialistic standpoint this would be the undesirable result of manufacturers giving up profits to their workmen.   Another point which Morris made in his defense was that even if workmen should receive all of the profits, they would not know how to spend their newly-acquired wealth.   They must be gradually educated to a higher standard of living.   It was desirable, first of all, that they should rise in culture and refinement; but this condition, he argued, could only be attained by their whole class rising.   The whole class could not rise, however, under the capitalistic system because competition keeps the standard down except under abnormal circumstances.   The socialistic capitalist, then, has this choice: shall he relieve his conscience by dividing a portion of his surplus value among his workers, or shall he continue to be a capitalist and use his money and his powers to further to the utmost a change in the structure of society?   If he can do both, so much the better; but if he cannot, it is right for him to keep his surplus value to further a great cause.   The third choice embodied in the biblical command: "If thou wilt be perfect, go, sell what thou hast, and give to the poor, and come, follow me," Morris thought of; but it seemed to him that this would practically mean abandoning the cause to live an ascetic life.

If these were ordinary times of peace, I might be contented amidst my discontent to settle down into an ascetic, such a man as I should respect even now.   But I don't see the peace or feel it: on the contrary, fate or what not has forced me to feel war, and lays hands on me as a recruit; therefore do I find it not only lawful to my conscience, but even compulsory on it, to do what in times of peace would not perhaps be lawful, and certainly would not be compulsory. If I am wrong, I am wrong; and there is an end of it.   Whatever hope or life there is in me is staked on the success of the cause. Of course I don't mean to say that I necessarily expect to see much of it before I die, and yet something I hope to see.[48]

From all this defense there can be no doubt that Morris believed that he was fully justified in continuing his business on the capitalistic basis and that he felt no real inconsistency between his practise and his social beliefs; yet it is difficult to see that the arguments which he advanced for his position are wholly consistent with his conviction that society was ripe for a new industrial era.   With his conclusion that it was his duty to devote his profits as well as himself to the one great cause which he had at heart, which certainly needed all the money it could get, there can be no manner of quarrel.   Yet it must be pointed out that though his conclusions are correct, his arguments are not wholly without fault. Consistency with his socialistic theories demanded that he transform his business into a coöperative productive association which would employ him as a director and manager.   It is to be remembered that Morris was not a State Socialist.   His statement that workmen must needs rise in culture and refinement before they could use intelligently the profits shared was not in accord with the hope Morris held at this time that society might be transformed in the very near future.   Entertaining such a hope, how could he believe that without refinement and culture, which takes years to develop, workers

[48]Mackail, II, 139.

could manage the new order in association with one another? Without due education they could no more use wisely the fruits of their labor and coöperation under a changed social structure than the profits which they might obtain from a socialistically inclined capitalist under the present system who would turn over his profits to them. It must be said, however, that Morris's disinclination to transform his business into a coöperative productive association was perfectly consistent with his later philosophy that people needed to be educated and socialized before they would be ready for the change which he advocated.

Still another alleged inconsistency charged against Morris is that he made articles in his shops which only the rich could afford to buy. To this Morris's reply would be the same as to the other accusations of hypocrisy made against him. The fault lay in the system, not in him. If conditions in the nineteenth century had been favorable to the production of beautiful things, no doubt Morris could have sold them more cheaply. But it must be remembered that the cost of producing a Morris work of art, whether it was wall-paper, or stained glass, or a piece of tapestry, was necessarily very high because he had to train his own workmen to do the work as it been done in mediaeval times.   In the Middle Ages, workmen knew the methods of work of the various trades in producing a piece of popular art; they had, as Morris often put it, a body of traditions to follow, besides having an inherited instinct which aided them in doing their skillful, artistic work; in the nineteenth century Morris had to deal with workmen who had no such traditions, no inherited instinct for good work. He himself had to master eight or nine crafts in order to put upon the market the artistic work which he and his workmen produced. The enormous cost of production of his wares, under nineteenth-century conditions was responsible, it might be urged, for the high prices he asked for them. Cheaper goods would have made necessary a lowering of the cost of production. This could only be done by mechanizing the work in some way; and to do this would not have accorded with Morris's ideas of allowing the workmen to express themselves in their products.   It would have taken away some of the pleasure of work, and to do this by any means whatsoever would be to lessen the value of the work as a piece of art. Morris maintained always that a piece of work should be made as well as it can be made to serve its purpose. And in following out this purpose, not only the worker, but the buyer is to be considered.   To make a product as excellent as it can be made gives the workman an opportunity to take a natural pride and to feel a natural satisfaction in his work; it gives him also a better remuneration for his product.   Not only are the interests of the worker cared for, but the buyer takes pleasure and derives a definite satisfaction from good work. Morris produced his goods at a necessarily high cost; that none but the rich could buy them was not his fault. He could consistently explain that if his workers were not given the "surplus value" that they produced, they could nevertheless have some share in the enjoyment of his artistic goods.

In this connection it is interesting to turn for a moment to Morris's workshops at Merton Abbey on the Wandle, to which place they had been moved in 1881.   From travelers' and visitors' descriptions of the plant a good idea may be obtained as to the conditions under which Morris's workmen labored.   He gave them an eight-hour day long before the Eight Hour agitation of the later eighties, and he paid them, as has before been pointed out, the highest wages known to their occupations.   M. Gabriel Mourey in an article on Morris & Company's workshops says:

The art workshops of Merton Abbey stand in an immense field amid tall trees and charming scenery.   Workshops, did I say? It is an ugly word that conjures up visions of grimy smoke, creaking machinery, and bodily toil.   No, there is nothing of all that. It is a sort of large farm-house built on one floor, surrounded by foliage and greenery, close by the bank of a small stream, the Wandle, which winds in and out with happy, joyous murmurs. Such is the workshop of Merton Abbey.   Nothing is manufactured except by hand.   No machine power is used, either steam or electric,

but implements of the simplest construction, the most primitive
in kind, the old tools, the old handicrafts of four or five hundred
years ago. *The predominant feature is that the artisan is allowed
almost perfect liberty of talent and imagination in the development of
his work.* This is especially the case in the tapestry and glass-work
studios where the most exquisite marvels of art are turned out.
The workman takes part in the work, becomes artist, and imparts
his own personality to the thing created, of which a rough plan has
first been drawn up by the master. The hand-press is used . . .
or the velvet and cretonne work is done directly with the hand.
Thus is avoided that monotonous stiffness peculiar to the work of
modern machinery, and further, it encourages the workman to
take a more personal interest in the labor.[49]

There are many other testimonials to the fact that
Morris's workshops were as unlike the ordinary business
factory as night the day. The rooms were well-lighted
and sunny; no crowding of either things or people, no
hurry of anyone. The making of money was not the
most requisite necessity in the manufacture of products
at Merton Abbey; "the genius of inventiveness and the
love of beauty are the ruling principles; . . . . no time,
trouble, or money is spared in making the work as perfectly true to the conception as human means can make
it. . . . The results are evolved out of individual choice.
. . . Here are examples of what the human machinery
can do at its best, heart, head, and hand, all in right
places relatively to one another."[50]

Morris's own workmen were too well pleased with
their master and his workshops ever to accuse him of
inconsistency because he was an employer of labor and
a Socialist at one and the same time. Criticism came
for the most part from those who did not understand
Socialism, but took it to be a system which demanded
that the rich should share their possessions equally with
the poor, a conception which many people still hold who
undertake to write articles on Morris's social thought.

The enormous energy and capacity for work which
enabled Morris to master many diverse arts and do distinguished work in them all was more than ever given
opportunity for expression in these years of devotion to

[49]Vallance, pp. 126-27. The italics are mine.
[50]Vallance, p. 130.

his new faith.   From February, 1885, to almost the end
of 1890, he managed the *Commonweal,* and contributed
numerous editorial notes, political notes, notes on passing events; in addition longer articles appeared such as
Attractive Labor, Feudal England; a long poem in thirteen
parts entitled *Pilgrims of Hope,* some sections of which
have marked literary value; the *Dream of John Ball;
Socialism, its Growth and Outcome,* written in conjunction
with E. Belfort Bax, and *News from Nowhere,* his utopian
romance.   At the same time he was lecturing about
England, was organizing branch societies of the Socialist
League, and was finding besides opportunities to attend
to his business as head of the firm, and to translate the
Odyssey.   In his capacity as a Socialist he sold pamplets
and other social literature; he spoke on street corners,
marched in processions along with workingmen, some
of whom hardly understood why they were marching
at all, or what it was they were trying to gain, save that
dimly they felt that they were unhappy and miserable,
while other people seemed happy and dwelt in plenty
and at ease.   Twice Morris was arrested and arraigned
in a police court.   Socialism, because of the great prominence it gained during the years of the eighties, irritated
the authorities, which declared, as a pretext for interfering with open-air meetings, that Socialists and their
audiences obstructed the thoroughfares.[51]

And indeed the government might well be interested.
Socialistic agitation was, at this time, exceptionally
favored by an industrial contraction of unusual character.
This circumstance naturally supplied Socialist lecturers
with an abundance of illustrative material.   The crisis
of 1878-79 had been followed by but a short and partial
recovery during 1881-83.   A period of prolonged depression followed, in which some of the staple trades
were subject to sudden and severe fluctuations.   In one
trade alone the fluctuation was so excessive that in one
year thousands of the most highly skilled and best organized mechanics were reduced to terrible destitution,
merely because of unprecedented over-production in
their trade.

[51]Vallance, pp. 336-37.

"In every shipbuilding port," wrote Mr. Robert Knight, in the Boilermakers' Annual Report of 1886, "there are to be seen thousands of idle men vainly seeking for an honest day's work. The privation that has been endured by them, their wives, and children, is terrible to contemplate. Sickness has been very prevalent, whilst the hundreds of pinched and hungry faces have told a tale of suffering and privation which no optimism can minimize or conceal. Hide it—cover it up as we may, there is a depth of grief and trouble the full revelations of which, we believe, cannot be indefinitely postponed. The workman may be ignorant of science and the arts, and the sum of his exact knowledge may be only that which he has gained in his close and circumscribed daily toil; but he is not blind, and his thoughts do not take the shape of daily and hourly thanksgiving that his condition is not worse than it is; he does not imitate the example of the pious shepherd of Salisbury Plain, who derived supreme contentment from the fact that a kind Providence had vouchsafed him salt to eat with his potatoes. He sees the lavish display of wealth in which he has no part. He sees a large and growing class enjoying inherited abundance. He sees miles of costly residences, each occupied by fewer people than are crowded into single rooms of the tenement in which he lives. He cannot fail to reason that there must be something wrong in a system which effects such unequal distribution of the wealth created by labor.[52]

At the International Trade-Union Congress of 1886 the leader of the Lancashire cotton-spinners, also a member of the Parliamentary Committee, speaking for the English section, said:

Wages had fallen, and there was a great number of unemployed. . . . Flax mills were being closed every day. . . . All the building trades were in a bad position; iron foundries were in difficulties, and one-third of the shipwrights were without work. . . . With a few exceptions, the depression affecting the great leading trades was felt in a thousand and one occupations. Seeing that there was a much larger number of unemployed, the question naturally presented itself as to whether there was no chance of improvement so long as the present state of society continued to exist. . . . He did not understand their Socialism; he had not studied it perhaps as he ought to have. The workmen of England were not so advanced as the workmen of the Continent. Nevertheless they, at least, possessed one clear conception; they realized that the actual producers did not obtain their share of the wealth they created.[53]

[52]Quoted from Sidney and Beatrice Webb, *History of Trade-Unionism*, pp. 364-5.
[53]Quoted from Webb, *History of Trade-Unionism*, p. 365. Emile de Laveleye, in *Contemporary Review*, March, 1890 (quoted in Dyer, *Evolution of Industry*), wrote: "The message of the 18th century to man was 'Thou shall cease to be the slave of nobles and despots who oppress thee; thou are free and sovereign.' It is a

A secretary of another union asked earnestly why Lord Dudley should inherit coal mines and land producing £1000 a day, while his colliers have to slave all the week and cannot get a living.[54]

But not alone was discontent caused by the unemployment and terrible destitution of large numbers of the workers; disclosure at this critical time by philanthropists of their experiences in looking over the sweated industries and the slums of the large cities added to the ferment. Middleclass attention was directed to the problems of the poor with an emphasis hitherto lacking, with the result that a great deal of money was contributed toward the amelioration of conditions. There was abundant cause for discontent, and discontent there was. Socialist teachings fell like a hot cinder on a mine of dynamite.

Trouble at Dod Street, 1885, and the interference of the police further caused intense excitement throughout London. It had long been the custom to hold open-air meetings at Dod Street. An order was summarily issued by the Government that these meetings must cease at once. The Socialists disregarded the order. A large crowd collected on the corner. The police, during the course of the meeting, charged on the people and arrested eight, Morris among them. The town, as a result, was in an uproar. People who were not even remotely interested in Socialism were greatly interested as Englishmen in their rights of free speech, which had been curtailed by the action of the authorities. Newspapers took up the matter with the result that the debate and discussion back and forth raised the Socialist League into an unhoped-for and unexpected popularity.

Precisely at this point in his activities Morris was attacked by the gout and compelled to leave the League for six weeks. Unfortunately for the cause so dear to his heart, his comrades in his absence fell to quarreling among themselves. Morris was greatly worried by

grand thing to be free and sovereign, but how is it that those who are held to be the source of power often cannot, even by hard work, provide themselves with the necessaries of life?"

[54]*Flint Glass Makers' Magazine*, November, 1884. Quoted from Sidney and Beatrice Webb, *History of Trade-Unionism*, p. 366.

this development. He knew that strong leadership
was needed and that he was the leader. His friends
used his illness as an opportunity to remonstrate with
him for giving so much of his precious energy to Socialism. Mrs. Burne-Jones was among those who tried
most emphatically to curb Morris's activities for the
League. Morris's answer to her letter is characteristic-
ally courageous:

You see, having joined a movement, I must do what I can while I
last; that is a matter of duty. . . . All this work I have pulled
upon my own head, and though in detail much of it is repulsive to
the last degree, I still hold that I did not do it without consideration. Anyhow, it seems to me that I can be of use; therefore I am
impelled to make myself useful.

It is true that I have no great confidence in the stability of our
party; but in the stability of the movement I have every confidence: and this I have always said to myself; that on the morrow
of the League breaking up, I and some half-dozen must directly
begin a new organization; and I believe we should do so.

You see, my dear, I cannot help it. The ideas which have taken
hold of me will not let me rest; nor can I see anything else worth
thinking of. How can it be otherwise, when to me society, which
to many seems an orderly arrangement for allowing decent people
to get through their lives creditably and with some pleasure, seems
mere cannibalism; nay, worse, (for there might be hope in that),
is grown so corrupt, so steeped in hypocrisy and lies, that one turns
from one stratum of it to another with hopeless loathing. One
must turn to hope and only in one direction do I see it — on the
road to Revolution: everything else is gone now.[55]

And a little later, after the quarrel within the League
had been made up, he wrote:

Even such things as this—the army setting out to conquer all the
world, turning back to burn Jack's pigstye, and tumbling drunk
into the fire—even this don't shake me: it means one must use the
best one can get; but one thing I won't do, wait forever till perfect
means are made for very imperfect me to work with. As to my
not looking round, why it seems to me that no hour of the day
passes that the whole world does not show itself to me.[56]

A large meeting of the unemployed on February 8,
1886, in Trafalgar Square and the riot which ensued
gave rise to the amazing hope in many Socialists that

[55]Mackail, II, 149-50.
[56]Mackial, II, 151.

the Revolution which was to change society was already at hand. Morris, however, saw more deeply into the situation. The *Commonweal* for March contains his thought as to what the steadfast policy of the Socialist League should be. That policy should be Education. The sort of aimless riot from which London had just suffered would, he said, happen again and again; it behooved the League to guard against the possible consequences of such incidents. The Gospel of Discontent was rapidly permeating the masses; the question for the League to answer was how that discontent should be used to bring about the reconstruction of society in accordance with their ideal. They could not hope of course that all of the workers could be educated in the thought of Socialism before more of such riots would take place; but they could at least hope that a large and strong group could be instructed in the economics, in the organization, and in the administration of the new order. Morris's plea against rioting was especially emphatic; he warned his readers that a counter-revolution would almost immediately sweep them away even if at first they were successful. He did not, however, countenance inaction when any really popular movement was in progress and when they as Socialists felt that they could at the same time make their own views perfectly clear. *Education toward Revolution*, or better worded, *The Reconstruction of Society* should be their policy in order that the Reconstruction might come with as little violence as possible.[57] Yet Morris held, despite the splendid moderation of his teaching, that if the upper classes pushed the masses into Revolution, the result must be good in the end, although the confusion and the misery attending it might be very great. But with planned riots as such he would have nothing whatever to do. If a riot were quite spontaneous, it would undoubtedly frighten the upper classes; but premeditated demonstrations, or shows of force, were absolutely useless unless they carried the opinions of all

[57]*Commonweal*, March, 1886.

of the people back of them, and as such, were then indications of real revolt.[58]

For the next two years, 1886-88, the details of Morris's
connection with the Socialist League are almost a repetition of the details just recounted. He continued
to spend an enormous amount of energy and time in
lecturing, and in writing editorials and articles for the
Commonweal. His hope in the near realization of the
Socialist ideal remained unchanged; indeed, he interpreted the signs of the times to mean that a great reconstruction of society was impending, although none
realized more fully than he that almost superhuman
patience would be needed to meet all of the irritating
worries that ever accompany great movements.   These
worries he felt to the full and expressed in a diary in
which he started to record the passing events connected
with the movement to which he was giving his deep
interest.   In these pages is revealed the wisdom which
time and experience were bringing him.   As he spent
his enthusiasm in expounding to his audiences of British
laboring men the aims and ideals of Socialism, he was
brought to the conclusion that they could not understand
fully those aims and ideals.   When he attacked the upper
classes, the interest of the workers would undoubtedly
be aroused; of their discontent he could have no manner
of doubt, nor of their class hatred; but of their comprehension of the gospel he was trying to bring them, he had
many misgivings.   It is not to be wondered, then, that
in his diary occur these words:

. . . the frightful ignorance and want of impressibility of the average
workman floors me at times. . . . The sum of it all is that the men
at present listen respectfully to Socialism, but are perfectly supine
and not in the least inclined to move except along the lines of Radicalism and Trades' Unionism. . . . I wonder sometimes if people
will remember in times to come to what depth of degradation the
ordinary English workman has been reduced.[59]

The apathy which Morris found thus discouraging in
the workingmen when he talked to them of the new
ideals which were to be their regeneration, also deterred

[58]Mackail, II, 175-6.
[59]Mackail, II, 172-74.

them from joining the branch organizations which the
Socialist League was endeavoring to found wherever
possible.   Morris of course readily perceived that a part
of their reluctance to allying themselves openly with a
party whose very name carried with it visions of red
flags and bombs and death (and still does even to many
of the educated to-day), was born of their fear of being
boycotted by their employers; the other part of their
reluctance arose from their dislike of organization and
of anything savoring of revolution.

In 1887 Morris wrote a little play entitled *The Tables
Turned, or Nupkins Awakened*, to be acted for the benefit
of the *Commonweal*.   It was produced in October, Morris
himself taking the part of the Archbishop of Canterbury.
G. Bernard Shaw said at the time that there was no
other such successful first night within memory.[60]   The
little playlet keenly satirized the understanding that
upper classes, especially the Judiciary, had of Socialism,
and the method in vogue of dealing out justice to the
rich and the poor.   The play brought home in addition
a very discouraging truth concerning the size of the
audiences which gathered to listen to the earnest words
of Socialist lecturers.   Briefly the plot runs thus: After
a trial of a respectable middle-class man for embezzle-
ment and a trial of a poor woman for stealing three
loaves of bread, there is called up a member of the
Socialist League, who is accused of obstructing the high-
way and inciting people to riot.   Several witnesses are
asked to testify, all of whom tell the most shamefully
perverted tales as to what the Socialist said in his
incendiary talk, and of the number present to hear him.
The Archbishop of Canterbury is then required to give
his testimony.   He admits that he was present at the
meeting, where, as he remembers, there were only four
people, including the speaker.   "I regret to have to say,"
continues the Archbishop, "that it was a mass of the
most frightful incendiarism, delivered with an occasional
air of jocularity and dry humor that made my flesh
creep.   Amidst the persistent attacks on property he

[60]Vallance, p. 334.

did not spare other sacred things. He even made an attack on my position, stating (wrongly), the amount of my moderate stipend." Lord Tennyson, another character, is also called as a witness; when asked if he could understand what the Socialist was saying, he answers: "No, I couldn't; I can't say I tried. I don't want to understand Socialism; it doesn't belong to my time." Just as the sentence of the prisoner to six years of penal servitude and a fine of £100 is pronounced, the Social Revolution, in which the Socialists, Morris among them, had such immediate hope, comes, and the tables are turned.[61]

A little more than a year and a half had passed since Morris had in the *Commonweal* discountenanced aimless riot, or even participation in revolt unless the workers really felt that a popular movement with a definite purpose was in progress.[62] The depression in industry in the year 1886 did not abate in 1887. The situation of the unemployed and their misery were very grave. English Radicals, not to mention Socialists, had long been aroused by the repressive measures of the Government directed against free speech. The Irish policy of the Ministry was the occasion of a meeting of all of those opposed to this and other measures of legislation, in Trafalgar Square, on Sunday, November 13, since named by history "Bloody Sunday". The members of the Radical Clubs in London, of the Irish National League, of the Social Democratic Federation, and of the Socialist League were united in the demonstration. A proclamation had been issued by the authorities prohibiting any meeting from being held in the Square and forbidding any organized procession to approach it. The order was not obeyed; and several clubs agreed to assemble at various specified places and join at the Square. Morris marched with the band that formed at Clerkenwell. The *Times'* report stated that both Morris and Mrs. Annie Besant were in the speakers' cart at Clerkenwell Green, and that both delivered speeches of

[61]Morris, *The Tables Turned, or Nupkins Awakened,* pp. 1-32.
[62]*Commonweal,* March, 1886.

a determined character. Morris, in particular, said that it was the duty of everyone to resist any attempt by whatever means in his power, to curtail the right of free speech. While the crowd from Clerkenwell was on its way to Trafalgar Square, it was attacked by the police and put to rout. The men, in utter disorder, nevertheless made their way to the Square as best they could, only to find that the other processions had fared as they had. The day was completely lost. The hopes of the Socialists that at least the beginning of the Revolution was at hand, were utterly dashed. Nothing was gained by this attempted demonstration. More than three hundred men were arrested. Some of these were imprisoned and fined; and others were condemned to penal servitude. Many were injured during the trouble, and three men were killed outright.[63] One of the victims was Alfred Linnell, whose funeral was the occasion of a large procession, and for whom Morris wrote a noble death-song.[64] He also made a speech at the grave. "Our friend who lies here," he said, "has had a hard life, and has met with a hard death; and if society had been differently constituted, his life might have been a delightful, a beautiful, and a happy one. It is our business to begin to organize for the purpose of seeing that such things shall not happen again; to try to make this earth a beautiful and happy place."[65]

For Morris the tragic termination of the Trafalgar Square meeting was decisive. The illusion that there was a great revolutionary force stirring in society and that the new order would come into being in his time, was swept away from his mind by the attempted meeting on "Bloody Sunday". With determined zeal he now returned to his former doctrine of Education toward Revolution. With that purpose in view he wrote indefatigably article after article for the *Commonweal*, explaining over and over the present basis of society, the antagonism of the classes, the uselessness of coöpera-

[63]Vallance, pp. 337-40.
[64]Morris, *Poems by the Way*, p. 36.
[65]Mackail, II, 192-93.

tion within a system of privilege, the reprehensible system of education prevalent, the helplessness of any philanthropic remedies for the wide-spread misery and actual degradation of the workers. His comments on the various strikes which were taking place in England in the later eighties made clear his opinion that though the strikes do not accomplish all that they set out to do, and though what they strive for is palliation (which Morris at this time rejected for the larger aims of Socialism) he nevertheless favored them rather than attempts to get labor reforms through Parliament. The strike, he held, is an education to the workers as to how to get larger things than Eight Hour days." Every strike, consequently, inspired him with fresh hope that the Gospel of Discontent, of Education toward Revolution was really advancing. As he studied the events of the day, it seemed to him that the strikers were actually awakening; that they felt that they were making war on capital.[67] The workers must realize, he taught, that they are practically slaves who desire and long for free-

[66]*Commonweal*, September, 1889.

[67]The great dock strike in London in August and September awakened much hope in Morris. Here Labor was organized for a definite end, and had an encouraging amount of public opinion of the better sort back of it. The strike was the result of an attempt to organize the unskilled laborers, an attempt which had been going on for some time. Socialistic doctrines had to some extent permeated this class. This condition, coupled with the fact that trade had been much depressed for several years, had led to efforts among the workers to organize. The strike of the match-girls in 1888 had aroused such sympathy as had never before been known. Subscriptions for their relief poured in from all sides. After two weeks of the strike, the employers were obliged to make some of the concessions asked for. This instance of unorganized, unskilled labor winning by force of public opinion taught a lesson to other unskilled workers, and concessions of a like kind were gained. This good example influenced the dock-workers; so under the influence of Tillet, Mann, and Burns, the great strike was managed successfully. As in the other cases just cited, public sympathy helped to win the day. The result of the strike was the formation of numbers of Trade Unions among the unskilled workers. (Sidney and Beatrice Webb, *History of Trade-Unionism*, pp. 388-91.) Morris hailed this strike with hope because of the sense of combination and power it gave to the men who participated. (Mackail, II, 224-25). He did not, however, realize its full import, or see for some time that the results of the new movement in the labor world were to turn the teachings of Socialism into constitutional channels. (Webb, p. 398).

The force of public opinion shown in these two historic strikes emphasizes the success of the Canadian Industrial Disputes Act. See Dr. Charles W. Eliot, *McClure's*, 30: 147 ff; Proceedings of the American Economic Association, 10: No. 1., Third Series, 158-79; United States Bulletin of Labor, 76 and also 86. For the text of the Act and comments upon its success, see Report of the Minister of Labor of Canada for the year ending March 31, 1910.

dom; that they can be freed; and finally, having learned all these things, they must enforce their will.[68]

Morris held fast to his old suspicion of Parliamentary action as a means to his ideal. Again and again he announced in the columns of the *Commonweal* that the League must succeed without Parliament. The policy of the League, as he put it, was abstention from all attempts to use the constitutional machinery of the government. His distrust of governmental action was founded upon the belief that the aim of Parliament was to uphold privilege and inequality. He forsaw, however, that the Socialists might need Parliament in the last act of the Revolution; they might by force of circumstances be obliged to make use of it to destroy the resistance of Reactionists. He had no faith that Parliament could even be led gently and by easy degrees into Socialism. It could be made to pass measures of amelioration for the condition of the poor, but for Socialists to accept these was, he believed, selling their birthright for a mess of pottage. The true weapon of the workers against Parliament was the boycott. Let Parliament alone, and meantime bend every energy to strengthen workers' organizations in order to deal directly with employers, and thus learn to be independent, to manage their own affairs. This was Morris's advice to the workers. The day of the general strike,—the strike which should usher in the new system,—was the day to keep ever in mind.[69] The lower classes *must*, Morris urged, wait for all that is worth having till people's minds are sufficiently impressed by the coming change to allow them to take definite and decided action.[70]

As time went on, the educational policy of Morris met with less and less approval from his colleagues in the Socialist League. The opposition to him was divided into two camps. The members of one group declared themselves in favor of palliatives and joined clubs which advocated such measures. In 1889 the Executive

[68]*Commonweal*, May 3, 1890.
[69]*Commonweal*, June 7, 1890.
[70]*Commonweal*, November 1, 1890.

Council of the Socialist League was captured by the other camp,—a group of men who had strong leanings toward Anarchism.   They alienated the more moderate members of the League and even deposed Morris from the control of the *Commonweal*.   With Anarchism Morris had no sympathy whatever.   To him, as a theory, it was destructive of the very idea back of the term *society*, for, as he said, it put man outside of it,—a position to Morris unthinkable and unimaginable.   Naturally the rebels of society were attracted to the anarchistic ideas.   The throwing of bombs by followers of this faith Morris thought to be a deplorable and regrettable disease; first, because of the method, and second, because it disgusted people and provoked the most hostile reaction.   As a matter of fact, he did not take the anarchists seriously.[71]   His views on Anarchism and his articles against it are all the more interesting when it is remembered that he has at various times been accused of being an anarchist, or at least of having leanings toward Anarchism.   This misapprehension has arisen because of the freedom he wished to leave each unit of society and each town.   With State Socialism he was entirely out of sympathy.

Morris was a delegate of the Socialist League to the Socialist Congress in 1889, and made one of the most effective of his speeches at the Congress.   But the Congress, as a whole, was a great disappointment to him. As is usual in a body of Socialists, there was endless discussion of the doctrines, differences of opinion as to ways and means, with no hope of agreement.   Morris left before the meeting was over, very little pleased, and very much discouraged by what he had seen and heard at the Congress.[72]

Despite the dissension in his organization and despite his deposition from the editorship of the *Commonweal*, Morris continued to contribute both money and articles to it, and bent every energy to keep the League together. His faith in the social ideals for which he worked never

[71] *Justice*, January 27, 1894.
[72] Vallance, pp. 348-49; Mackail, II, 224.

wavered; but as time went on, his hope in the near triumph of his beliefs became feebler. Finally, Morris felt that he could no longer remain in the League. His last article entitled *Where are we Now?* appeared in the *Commonweal* for November 15, 1890. When he left, Morris said that he could not work with Anarchists who advocated the barricading of London. The Socialist League itself came to an end in 1892. It had followed the fate of the International and for similar reasons.[73]

In Morris's last contribution to the *Commonweal*, he reviewed the Socialist movement of the eighties during its brief history of seven years and expressed the opinion that few movements had made so much progress in so short a time, considering the large aim which the founders had in mind; no less an aim than to change the system of society on which is founded the whole of civilization. "Could seven years," asked Morris," make any visible impression on such a tremendous undertaking as this?

Consider, too, the quality of those who began and carried on the this business of reversing the basis of modern society. A few workingmen, less successful even in the wretched life of labor than their fellows; a sprinkling of the intellectual proletariat, whose keen pushing of Socialism must have been pretty certain to extinguish their limited chances of prosperity; one or two outsiders in the game political; a few refugees from the bureaucratic tyranny of foreign governments; and here and there an impractical, half-cracked artist or author. Yet such as they were, they were enough to do something. Through them, though not by them, the seven years of the new movement toward freedom, had contrary to all that might have been expected, impressed the idea of Socialism deeply on the epoch. . . . When I first joined the Socialist movement, I hoped that some workingman leader, or rather leaders, would turn up who would push aside all middle-class help and become great historical figures. I might still hope for that, if it seemed likely to happen, for indeed, I long for it enough; but to speak plainly, it does not seem so at present. Yet, I repeat, in spite of all drawbacks, the impression has been made, and why? . . . because that seemingly inexpugnable fabric of modern society is verging toward its fall; it has done its work, and is going to change into something else.

So much at least we have to encourage us. But are not some of us disappointed in spite of the change, at the way in which Socialism is looked on generally? It is but natural that we should be.

[73]Mackail, II, 230-32, 237.

When we first began to work together, there was little said about anything save the great ideals of Socialism; and so far off did we seem from the realization of these, that we could hardly think of any means for their realization, save great dramatic events, which would make our lives tragic indeed, but would take us out of the sordidness of the so-called "peace" of civilization.   With the great extension of Socialism, this also is changed.   Our very success has dimmed the great ideals that first led us on; for the hope of the partial, and so to say, vulgarized realization of Socialism is now pressing on us.   I think that we are all confident that Socialism will be realized; it is not wonderful, then, that we should long to see—to feel—its realization in our own lifetime.   Methods of realization, therefore, are now more before our eyes than ideals: but it is of no use talking about methods which are not, in part at least, immediately feasible, and it is of the nature of such partial methods to be sordid and discouraging, though they *may* be necessary.

There are two tendencies in this matter of methods: on the one hand is our old acquaintance, palliation, elevated now into vastly greater importance than it used to have, because of the growing discontent, and the obvious advance of Socialism: on the other hand is the method of partial, necessarily futile, inconsequent revolt, or riot rather, against the authorities who are our absolute masters and can easily put us down.

With both of these methods I disagree: and that the more because the palliatives have to be clamored for, and the riots carried out by men who do not know what Socialism is, and have no idea what their next step is to be, if contrary to all calculation they should happen to be successful.   Therefore, at the best our masters would be our masters still, because there would be nothing to take their place.   *We are not ready for* such a change as that! . . . Before I write a very few words on the only line of method on which some of us can work, I will give my views about the present state of the movement as briefly as I can.

The whole set opinion amongst those more or less touched by Socialism, who are not definite Socialists, is towards the new Trades' Unionism and palliation.   Men believe that they can wrest from the capitalists some portion of their privileged profits, and the masters, to judge by the recent threats of combination on their side, believe that this can be done.   That it could only very partially be done, and that the men could not rest there if it were done, we Socialists know very well; but others do not.

I neither believe in State Socialism as desirable in itself, nor indeed, as a complete scheme do I think it possible.   Nevertheless some approach to it is sure to be tried, and to my mind, this will precede any complete enlightenment on the new order of things. The success of Mr. Bellamy's Utopian book, deadly dull as it is, is a straw to show which way the wind blows.   The general attention paid to our clever friends, the Fabian lecturers and pamphleteers, is not altogether due to their literary ability; people have really got their heads turned more or less in their direction.

Now it seems to me that at such a time, when people are not only discontented, but have really conceived a hope of bettering the condition of labor, while at the same time the means toward their end are doubtful; or rather when they take the very beginning of the means as an end in itself,—at this time when people are really excited about Socialism, and when many who know nothing about it think themselves Socialists, is the time of all others to put forward the simple principles of Socialism, regardless of the policy of the passing hour. . . . I say for us *to make Socialists is the business* at present, and at present I do not think we can have any other useful business. Those who are not really Socialists—who are Trades' Unionists, disturbance-breeders, or what not,—will do what they are impelled to do, and we cannot help it. At the worst there will be some good in what they do; but we need not and cannot work heartily with them, when we know their methods are beside the right way.

Our business, I repeat, is the making of Socialists, i.e., convincing people that Socialism is good for them and is possible. When we have enough people of that way of thinking, *they* will find out what action is necessary for putting their principles in practice. Therefore, I say, make Socialists. We Socialists can do nothing else that is useful. [74]

Dreamer of dreams, Morris saw a vision of the ideal, and could not bear to give up the ultimate aim for a few present gains. To him that course meant the dimming of first principles. With a curious blindness he failed to realize at this period that every gain which raises the standard of life among the workers would also raise them spiritually and educationally, and thus, in a sense, his ultimate ideals for man's happiness, for a *Menschenwürdiges Dasein*, would be fulfilled, and the goal of Socialism brought nearer. But until men are Socialists, said Morris, there can be no reign of Socialism. To some measure of this view Morris held to the end, although he came to see—for he had an intensely practical side—more of good in the measures for the amelioration of the lot of the poor.

In an interview published in *Justice* for January 27, 1894, Morris was reported to have spoken thus:

[74]*Commonweal*, November, 1890.

I think Socialism has made more progress than we know—more than we anticipated ten years ago. It shows that these ideas were already in the air. Anyway, they are now becoming popular. . . . The people will not revolt until every means have been tried, and even if they did, they would be mowed down to a man by the machine guns and the rifles of the soldiery. . . . Political means are the only ones available at present. I think we have to create a party. A party with delegates in the House of Commons which would have complete control over those delegates would rapidly grow. An isolated member in Parliament is apt to backslide, but not a party and delegates. The party of reaction would make concession after concession until it was forced over the edge, and then they would probably surrender with discretion. This has been the history of most popular movements in this country. You cannot start with revolt; you must lead up to it, and exhaust other means first. I do not argue that you should abstain from an act merely on the ground that it would precipitate civil war, even though the result of civil war were problematical, so long as the initial act were justifiable. But with the tremendous power of modern armies it is essential that everything essential should be done to legalize revolt. The soldiers will fire upon the people without hesitation so long as there is no doubt as to the legality of doing so. Men do not fight well with halters around their necks, and that is what a revolt would mean. We must try and gain a position to legalize a revolt.

Present circumstances, it seems to me, go to prove the wisdom of the Social Democratic Federation in drawing up that list of palliative measures, that contemporary program,[75] as one may call

[75]The palliatives urged by the Federation were as follows:

1. The compulsory construction of healthy dwellings for the people: such dwellings to be let at rents to cover the cost of construction and maintenance alone.

2. Free secular and technical education, compulsory upon all classes, together with free maintenance for the children in all board schools.

3. Eight hours or less for the normal working day, fixed in all trades and industries by legislative enactment, and not more than forty-eight hours a week, penalties to be inflicted for any infringement of this law.

4. Cumulative taxation of all incomes exceeding £300 a year.

5. State appropriation of railways; municipal ownership and control of gas, electric light, and water supplies; the organization of tramways and omnibus services and similar monopolies in the interests of the entire community.

6. The extension of the post-office savings bank, which should absorb all private institutions that derive a profit from operations in money or credit.

7. Repudiation of the national debt.

8. Nationalization of the land, and organization of agricultural and industrial armies under state and municipal control on a coöperative basis.

As means of the peaceful attainment of these objects the Social Democratic Federation advocated:

Payment of members of Parliament and all local bodies and official expenses of elections out of the public funds. Adult suffrage. Annual Parliaments. Proportional representation. Second ballot. Abolition of the monarchy and the House of Lords. Disestablishment and disendowment of all State churches. Extension of the power of County Councils. The establishment of District Councils. Independent legislation for all parts of the empire.—*Justice*, (any number).

it. Mean and paltry, as it seemed to me, and does still, as compared with the whole thing, something of the kind is absolutely
essential.

The deep disappointment of seeing the Socialist
League, which he had founded, break to pieces before
his eyes, of learning that he was not safe even from
harsh criticism in the *Commonweal*, which he had fi-
nanced for more than five years, and most of all, of
realizing that his motives were misunderstood within
his own circle, did not discourage William Morris. He
had been disillusioned many times during the seven
years of his connection with the Socialist movement.
Several popular risings in which he had taken part and
from which he had hoped great things for society had
failed; but from them he learned that his ideal would
never be realized in his lifetime; that the system of
society which the centuries have built up cannot be
annihilated in a day by premature revolution,—systems
too must evolve. Encounters with the police taught
him that militant measures were not the best way of
accomplishing results. But to make Socialists remained
his aim; he held fast to this conclusion to the end. As
he had written to Mrs. Burne-Jones in 1886, that "on
the morrow of the League breaking up I and some half-
dozen must directly begin a new organization,"[76] so he
did in 1890. He formed, with a small number of friends
who seceded from the League with him, the Hammersmith Socialist Society. A local branch of the League
had been established at Hammersmith some years before.
This little branch society Morris and his friends reorganized. The hall which the society used was one
attached to his own home on the upper Mall. There
on every Sunday evening, and sometimes during the
week, in the years from 1890 to 1896, Morris and his
colleagues might be found talking over theories of Art
and Life.[77] Public campaigning Morris abandoned;
but he abandoned it not because, as many of his critics
say, he saw that he had given his time and strength to a

[76]Mackail, II, 150.
[77]Vallance, pp. 356-57.

lost cause, but because he believed that the making of
Socialists could not be carried on by conflicts with the
police or by other means that drew forth the disappro-
bation of law-abiding and peace-loving citizens.   It is
William Morris's distinction that he always acted on
his beliefs.   When he thought that the happiness of the
race might be brought about in his lifetime, because the
people, as it appeared to him, were ready for the Revolution, he was ready to assist by militant means, if necessary,
—and for a moment it had appeared to him to be
necessary,—in the establishment of a new system of
society; when he saw, after seven years spent in devotion
to the cause, that he had been mistaken in the belief
that the regeneration was at hand, he took up the creed
which he enunciated in the last article he wrote for the
Commonweal, and prepared to live it himself.   This he
did.   The failures and disillusionments of the past years
had no power to daunt him.

The breach with Mr. Hyndman and the Social
Democratic Federation was closed in the period from
1890 to 1896.   Morris contributed poems to *Justice* on
several occasions, and also several articles on Socialism.
His last contribution to *Justice* appeared on May Day,
1896, six months before his death.   A study of his last
utterances on Socialism reveal the fact that he had
practically come to the point of view of the Fabian
Society and of others whom he had formerly called
Opportunists,—that there was some value in doing
things to relieve the workers under the present system.[78]
G. Bernard Shaw testifies that Morris's last important
act in the Socialist movement was to try to unite all of
the Socialist Societies into a single party, and that he did
his utmost to bring about this result.   He did not, however, succeed in effecting a union.   He lectured from
time to time for the Social Democratic Federation at
its branch associations, and spoke earnestly and emphatically for its Parliamentary candidates.   The last
public lecture outside of his own society was given for
the Social Democratic Federation on New Year's Day,

[78]Vallance, p. 357.

1896, in Holburn Town Hall. His words there were so enthusiastically received that he felt at last that Socialism was being comprehended by the very men whom he had always wished to reach.[79]

In following out the history of Morris's connection with Socialism, the work which he did in art and literature has necessarily slipped into the background. During all of these years Morris had also lectured on Art, its theory, and its relation to life. Mention has already been made of his preaching of his social ideals in connection with lectures on Art. His practice of the arts and his teaching of their principles bore immediate fruit in the formation about Morris of a group of artists and craftsmen who set for their aim the regeneration of all of the arts of life. They were not all Socialists, but they all held social ideals of one sort or another; and though their lines of work were diverse, it is asserted that Morris had been the dynamic influence upon them all. Morris's practice in his own workshops had followed two leading principles: first, that all work done in his shops he should know how to do himself; and second, that all decorative art should be done with reference to architecture, the mistress-art of all arts. These principles were carried out both within the workshop and in the formation of guilds and associations. The Art Workers' Guild was established in 1884, out of which grew the Arts and Crafts Exhibition Society a little later.[80]

In literature he was no less active. He had begun translating the Odyssey in 1886. *The Dream of John Ball*, in some ways the most striking of his prose works, was written the next year, and published in the *Commonweal;* two months later he published *Signs of Change*, a volume which contains most of his exposition of Socialism. *The House of the Wolfings* was begun immediately after, inaugurating a long series of prose romances.

[79]Vallance, p. 358.
[80]Mackail, II, 194-98.

About 1889 Morris began to be increasingly interested in typography, to which art his attention was directed by his neighbor, Emery Walker.   Morris had collected many of the earliest printed books, but principally because of their woodcuts.   His interest in typography culminated in the establishment of the Kelmscott Press. What Morris tried to do in mastering the art of printing was to go back to the time when that art was following the right principles and to develop it from that point.   He succeeded by his efforts in this field in producing work of a beauty and excellence altogether unknown since the first half of the sixteenth century.   It is not too much to say that he revolutionized the art of printing.   But the Kelmscott Press was the last undertaking Morris was permitted to begin.   In 1895 his health began to fail, and on the third of October, 1896, he passed away.

Even before Morris's death, events were forming themselves toward a working out to some degree of his social hopes.   Kier Hardie, in 1893, had formed the Independent Labor Party.   In 1900 the Labor Representative Committee (trade union), the Social Democratic Federation, the Independent Labor Party, and Fabian Society joined hands; and in 1906, only ten years after the death of Morris, this coalition, (minus the Social Democratic Federation), became the Labor Party, which in union with the Liberals brought about a transformed Great Britain.   In this Labor Party Great Britain achieved Morris's last aim—a united social democracy.

PART III

THE
SOCIAL IDEALS OF WILLIAM MORRIS

CHAPTER I

THE RELATION OF ART TO LIFE

It never occurred to William Morris, as it does to many so-called practical people, to ask whether art is worth the serious consideration of serious men. Endowed by nature with a passion for the beautiful, the words of Ruskin on the vital importance and relation of art to humankind, which he heard when he was an undergraduate at Oxford, Morris found to be the words of a prophet and a seer. From Ruskin he learned that art is the expression of the soul of a God-made man,[1] and that national art depends upon national character. "Let a nation be healthy, happy, pure in its enjoyments," Ruskin wrote, "brave in its acts, and broad in its affections, and its art will spring round and within it as freely as the foam from a fountain; but let the springs of its life be impure, and its course polluted, and you will not get the bright spray by treatises on the mathematical structure of bubbles."[2] Ruskin really taught Morris the laws of constructive art and the dependence of all human work for its beauty on the happy life of the workman;[3] in other words, he taught Morris the relation of art to life. Yet in Morris's long years of practical touch with the handicrafts, the ideas which he accepted from Ruskin gained a color quite their own. More than this, they became dynamic, both in his own life and in the lives of others. And it is the distinction of William Morris's words on the relation of art to life that they are not only still dynamic, but they are even more dynamic now than in his lifetime.

Numberless times in his writings does Morris explain his idea of art. "That thing which I understand by real art," he wrote, "is the expression by man of his pleasure in labor."[4] "Art is the beauty of life."[5] "What

[1]Ruskin, *Modern Painters*, III, 147-48.
[2]Ruskin, *On the Old Road*, I, 227.
[3]Ruskin, *Stones of Venice*, II, 159-75.
[4]Morris, *Hopes and Fears for Art*, p. 58.
[5]*Ibid.*, p. 75.

I mean by art is some creation of man which appeals to his emotions and his intellect by means of his senses."[6] "Art, is the divine solace of human labor, the romance of each day's hard practise of the difficult art of living."[7] To Morris, art is the cause of the true pleasure and happiness of life.[8] In most of these dicta it is clear that Morris emphasized the artist, the *man*. Art makes labor pleasurable; it brings happiness to the user, but most of all to the maker. Morris's whole social doctrine sprang from his firm belief that art is the expression of man's joy in his labor. In his philosophy the relation of art to life is one of the most intimate and the most necessary of relations, for he believed that the happiness of men depends upon the kind of work they do, and the freedom with which they are allowed to do it.

Morris was very careful, however, to distinguish real art from sham art. Only the product that results from self-expression is real art.[9]

Men whose hands were skilled in fashioning things [wrote Morris] could not help thinking the while, and soon found out that their deft fingers could express some part of the tangle of their thoughts, and that this new pleasure hindered not their daily work, for in the very labor that they lived by lay the material in which their thought could be embodied; and thus, though they labored, they labored somewhat for their pleasure, and uncompelled, and had conquered the curse of toil, and were men.[10]

Real Art is the product of the untramelled worker. It is not the result of a conscious striving for beauty merely for the sake of beauty; for man's instinct for beauty causes him unconsciously to make things beautiful. To make things beautiful for the sake of beauty is likely to produce, in the opinion of Morris, work that shows affectation and effeminacy.

In the great times of art, conscious effort was used to produce great work for the glory of the city, the triumph of the Church, the exaltation of the citizens, the quickening of the devotion of the faith-

[6]Morris, *Architecture, etc.*, p. 38.
[7]*Ibid.*, p. 110.
[8]*Ibid.*, pp. 115-22.
[9]*Ibid.*, p. 32.
[10]Morris, *Architecture*, etc., p. 39.

ful; even in the higher art, the record of history, the instruction of men alive and to live hereafter, was the aim rather than beauty.[11]

Sham art, on the other hand, Morris explained, is the mechanical substitute for real art.[12] It is the so-called art which is produced by mechanical means, the ornament which is added to an article by machinery. Since machinery is a modern invention, sham art is a modern production. Its effect on civilization is three-fold. First, it works the effect of all shams and untruths; second, since it can be made cheaply in unlimited quantities by the never-wearied machine, it tends to drive out real art; and third, it destroys appreciation of real art. The displacement of real art means that man is deprived of an opportunity for free self-expression in his work. It follows logically, therefore, from Morris's theory of art, that when sham art is the rule, man has but little chance of happiness.[13]

Perhaps Morris's position on this point needs more explanation. A machine necessarily presupposes an operative,—a person who swings a lever, who guides a needle, who turns a thumb-screw, one who repeats the same turn of his hand or foot over and over many times a day for all of the years of his life. His main thought and attention is given, not to the product of the machine, but to the machine itself. If the machine is properly run, it turns out ornament with perfect mechanical finish and with unerring adjustment of part to part. The ornament applied to the product has not been planned in the brain of the operative; its every curve does not show the thrill and inspiration of his creating mind. The creative thrill has been enjoyed by the designer alone. Ideas may indeed teem in the brain of the tender of the machine; yet he must merely turn the lever or guide the needle; the machine can make only what it has been invented to make. For want of expression the thoughts of the operative must therefore die in his brain. Here is a sinful waste of human thought,

[11]*Ibid.*, pp. 221-22.
[12]Morris, *Hopes and Fears for Art*, p. 213.
[13]*Ibid.*, p. 213.

of human power, capable under right conditions of almost infinite development, capable of enriching life, of making life happy.

But this is not the whole story.   For not often does the operative have even the joy of tending an intricate machine which turns out the whole of the article; for most machines nowadays make but part of an article. Division of labor and the continued invention of machinery have been carried so far that usually machines are comparatively simple.   They make a tenth or sometimes a hundreth part of the whole product.   It may be said with truth that the management and care of a complicated machine is capable of stimulating the imagination and demanding high skill from the operative, perhaps leading him on to further invention; but this cannot be true in the same degree at least of a simple mechanism exacting no skill in care and attention, and making but an infinitesimal part of an article.   In addition, extreme division of labor prevents the operative from thinking of the product as a whole.   The finished piece cannot be his concern.   His work is narrowed to his small duty.   And indeed, the less he thinks, the swifter will he work.   The modern system naturally does not encourage him to think and dream about what he might add of beauty and finish to an article were he making the whole.   The designer of the product and the inventor of the machine have monopolized all of the work-pleasure.

What is the result, then, upon the maker, of being obliged to produce machine-made ornament, or, as Morris put it, sham art?   It will readily be granted that the disuse of a faculty or a member usually means the atrophy of that faculty or member.   When one is not allowed to express one's thoughts in creative work, one is likely to lose the power of doing creative work.   Too much drudgery of a purely mechanical kind in the end kills the creative impulse.   The exercise of the creative impulse Morris firmly believed, brings man, in the truest sense of the word, his greatest happiness in life.

When he is not permitted to use the creative energy within him, he loses his greatest source of pleasure.

Morris taught also that not only is the maker injured by the lack of expression of his ideas, but the user suffers along with him. The user suffers because he is deprived of the uplifting influence of contemplating works that express brain-power, inspiration, beauty, soul.[14] His imagination is not stirred by the perfection and polish of the machine-made product, for an article made in such a way has no human and cultural influence upon him.[15] He may exclaim in wonder at the mechanical ingenuity of the inventor of the machine; he may admire the brain-power of the designer as expressed in the whole article; and yet at the same time he may condemn his taste. He cannot, however, read the happy thought-life of the workman in the machine-made wares. He can, if he is a thinker and a student of social conditions, read the maker's soul-death and consequent unhappiness.

It is necessary before following Morris's reasoning further on this point to consider another of his classifications of art. He divides real art into two classes: great art and popular art. The creation of great art depends on the artist's superior endowment of high and serious imagination. For this reason great art appeals especially to the imagination. This does not mean that it is created for the few, or that it should be carefully kept for the few; for everyone, if he has not been deprived of it by defective education, has some imagination.[16] By defective education Morris meant an education which excludes people from understanding art; right education being such as allows them to practise art for themselves. The power of great art, he said, is vastly stronger if it be the blossom of all the half-conscious or popular art below it;[17] that is to say, if all are left free to practise art. Under such conditions its great purpose of feeding the minds and souls of all people, of training their intellects, of exciting

[14]Morris, *Architecture*, etc., p. 170.
[15]Morris, *Hopes and Fears for Art*, p. 213.
[16]Morris, *Architecture*, etc., p. 38.
[17]Morris, *Hopes and Fears for Art*, p. 77.

their emotions, and of pleasing their senses is fulfilled.[18]
If it stands alone, unsupported by and separated from
the art of the people, its beneficent social influence cannot be exerted; consequently, the artist's great gift is
wasted.

Popular art also demands imagination, but imagination of a lower type. This is the only essential difference
between the two kinds of art. Morris analysed popular
art thus: It rises out of the wants and desires of men
which have to be satisfied by the organized labor of the
people. It includes a large variety of industries; for
example, the crafts of house-building, painting, joinery,
carpentry, smiths' work, pottery, and glass-making.[19]
These supply some of the material needs of mankind,—
needs, it is true, which can be supplied by merely useful
products expressing no imagination and having no
ornament. The records of history, however, show that
man has not been satisfied with merely useful things,
for many of the ancient articles of daily use which have
come down to modern times prove that they have embodied the highest aspirations of their makers.[20] This
soul-expression of the people shows itself in added ornament, in variation in form and color. The worker who
produces wares with the idea that they are to express
his heart and soul, perhaps unconsciously, but entirely
untramelled, is as inevitably producing a work of art
as the great artist who interprets his soul and records
his aspirations in painting or sculpture. The difference
between the artist and the maker, let it be repeated,
resides in the difference between their imaginations,
and this is merely a difference of degree. The two
types of art are alike in four respects: both must show
the hand as guided by the brain; both must secure results naturally from the material in hand, and further
must be suited to the material to the degree that the
same result could be obtained through no other medium;
both must show a love of nature in all its forms to the

[18]Morris, *Architecture*, etc., p. 166.
[19]Morris, *Hopes and Fears for Art*, p. 3.
[20]Morris, *Architecture*, etc., pp. 38-39. See also Professor John R. Commons'
article on *Utilitarian Idealism*.

extent that this love be the dominant spirit; and both
must be guided by a sound, hopeful, original brain so
alive to its environment that that environment shall be
interpreted in the work.[21]   By original Morris meant
that both popular art and great art should imitate old
forms no more than may be necessary, although he recognized that it is impossible not to impress something
of the past history of an art upon its present practise
even while the life of the day also finds impression in it.
The reason for this is that the form used must either
be a development or a degradation of that in vogue
generations ago.[22]

Morris's analysis of great and lesser art indicates the
high esteem in which he held the latter.   He recognized,
of course, the superiority of great art; but he was always
more interested in the art of the people, that art which
clusters about their attempts to make life more interesting and more pleasant.   His study of the remains of
ancient and mediaeval art proved to him that the power
to produce lesser art was universal, and that the will to
produce it, although it added more work to the already
over-burdened people, was also universal.

An inquiry into the question as to why people have
not been satisfied to make merely useful articles un-
adorned by fancy or expression of individuality, when
such adornment adds to the necessary labor of mankind, led Morris to an analysis of the moods which sway
men.   Man is dominated, he said, by two moods: a
mood of energy, and a mood of idleness.   He is ruled
by first one mood and then by the other; and whichever is
uppermost demands imperatively the satisfaction of
its kind.   If anything interferes with the exercise of the
kind of activity which a mood requires, certainly rest-
lessness, and perhaps a degree of unhappiness results.
When, for example, the mood of energy predominates,
and man is free to express it, he must be doing something;
he must be making something, or be pretending to make
it.   And because he expects to achieve some precon-

[21]Morris, *Architecture*, etc., p. 43.
[22]Morris, *Hopes and Fears for Art*, pp. 7-8.

ceived result, the mood of energy is hopeful and pleasureful. If he sets out to carve a chest or to weave a tapestry, he generally has some definite idea of what he wants to do; he enjoys the growing of his work before his eyes; and further, he anticipates pleasure from its use. To exercise the mood of energy without hope of achievement, without freedom of individual action, is destructive of the joy and happiness which all work should bring. This is what is happening under the modern system. Work is no longer untrammelled, for the machine and and division of labor rule; the mood of energy cannot therefore be exercised under conditions which produce inspired work,—inspired and inspiring both for the maker and the user. Each one can attest the truth of Morris's analysis by studying his own experience with work. Given the knowledge of the technique of a craft, material to work with, leisure to work in, a whole piece of work to do, and the right conditions obtain for happy work,—which is inspired, individual, hopeful, expressive of the worker's fancy. According to the definition of Morris, work done under such conditions is real art.

It has been stated that a maker producing wares under conditions outlined in the preceding paragraph puts more labor into them than is required to make them serve merely the purpose for which they were produced. A free worker unconsciously adds ornament, and this certainly increases his labor. Why does he voluntarily take infinite pains to add that to merely useful articles which makes them works of art? Because, Morris answered, it gives him pleasure,—sensuous pleasure to make them thus, and anticipated pleasure for the user, whether he or some other use them.[23] The freedom to produce works of art takes the sting of slavery out of dull work; it turns labor from dogged endurance into pleasure.[24]

Morris's analysis of work-pleasure will further clarify the matter under discussion. Emphatically the pleasure which comes with the creation of art is based on the

[23]Morris, *Signs of Change*, pp. 117-31.
[24]Morris, *Hopes and Fears for Art*, pp. 4-6.

keen interest which a healthy man takes in healthy
life. It has four elements: first, variety; second, hope
of creation; third, the self-respect born of a sense of
usefulness; and fourth, the sensuous delight which accompanies the skilful exercise of bodily powers. Three
of these elements need no further explanation; the
naming of them is sufficient. Concerning the second,
the hope of creation, a word may be said. Morris
meant by this the hope of producing worthy work which
but one craftsman could make. In other words, he
meant individual work, because no two souls are alike
in the world, no two have identical individualities.
Real art is therefore always individual.[25]

From his studies of the art-treasures of antiquity,
Morris found additional evidence that work rightly
done under right conditions brought pleasure. The most
primitive and rudest races made in their pottery images
of fishes, birds, and other animal forms and of nature
about them long before drawing or any rules of drawing
developed. The craftsmen of the Dark Ages and later
transmitted their thoughts and dreams to the materials
upon which they worked. Their work also was the
expression of what they saw and felt of the life and
ideas about them. All this indicated to Morris what he
found to be true in his own art-work,—that creation is
a need of the human soul, and that such creation causes
real happiness.[26]

Morris considered it a kind and a beneficent gift of
nature that since most people must work, work rightly
pursued can and does and should bring pleasure. Even
animals feel a degree of the same kind of pleasure which
man feels in untrammelled activity. The fish delights
to swim, the bird to fly, even though they do so in
search of food.[27] Morris's analysis shows that he saw
deeply into fundamentals. He has expressed in un-
scientific terms what Jacques Loeb, in his *Physiology of
the Brain*, states in the language of his science.

[25]Morris, *Architecture*, etc., pp. 176-77.
[26]*Ibid.*, p. 119.
[27]Morris, *Hopes and Fears for Art*, pp. 58-9.

Human happiness is based upon the possibility of a natural and harmonious satisfaction of the instincts. One of the most important instincts is usually not even recognized as such; namely the instinct of workmanship. Lawyers, criminologists, and philosophers frequently imagine that only wants make one work. This is an erroneous view. We are forced to be active in the same way as ants or bees. The instinct of workmanship would be our greatest source of happiness if it were not for the fact that our present social and economic organization allows only a few to gratify this instinct.[28]

Morris's study of the art of all ages led him to the conclusion that since the modern system is what it is, only a few workmen can really be happy in their work. Their daily work lacks the pleasure of creation, for they are mere tenders of machines. This conclusion stares the reader in the face on almost every page of Morris's voluminous writings. Nowhere is Morris hesitant in his utterance: the workman whose daily work lacks pleasure cannot be happy; for real, satisfying happiness cannot be found elsewhere than in congenial, free work.[29] But in his eagerness to demonstrate the joyless life of the modern workman, Morris forgot perhaps that the void made in the lives of millions by denying them expression of their natural instincts can be at least partly filled by teaching workers the lesson of thorough work, and managers the lesson of appreciating thorough work in their subordinates, and of the beauty and wisdom of voicing such appreciation in appropriate ways. For instance, the college boy cleaning street-lamps may detest his work; but if he is a good worker, he finds pleasure in the brightness of his lamps. The superintendent of a shop may add to the pleasure of his workers and to the efficiency of his factory by inviting and rewarding valuable suggestions as to how the work may be better carried on. Furthermore, in many instances a worker will find pleasure in working on something that is the best of its kind or is highly useful, rather than upon something made merely to sell. The farmer trying to produce the best stock, or the child striving

[28]Jacques Loeb, *Comparative Physiology of the Brain*, p. 309. See also p. 197.
[29]Morris, *Architecture*, etc., pp. 221-22.

for the best ear of corn are other examples.   Pure-food
and other investigators have pointed out some of the ill
effects on the consumer of dishonest products; but
there is also social loss which grows out of the moral
degradation of the worker who continually turns out
immoral products.   Good citizenship is imperilled by a
tolerance of any production that offers poor goods.   This
is a point which Morris always emphasized.   The works
of men, in his opinion, cannot show a mere negation of
beauty; if they are not beautiful, and therefore cultural
and elevating, they are undisguisedly ugly, and therefore degrading.   More than this, he believed that the
ugliness of unbeautiful work is a dynamic ugliness; for
it causes a progressively spiritual deterioration, at last
pushing man to such depths that he is not even conscious of his degradation, and blatantly refuses to see
anything serious or worth while in art or beauty.   When
such a condition becomes general, real progress stops
and the intellectual death of the race is at hand.   Art
is therefore necessary to the spiritual growth of mankind.[30]

The exposition of Morris's theory of the relation of
art to life has thus far been confined to the individual;
there still remains the consideration of society. Morris's
art-theory is partly based on the art-remains of older
ages, and partly on his analysis of his own experience
and that of brother-artists. Not only, said Morris,
does man tell the story of his hopes and fears, of the
aspirations of his soul toward God and the ideal in the
work which he produces; but since man cannot be imagined outside of society, it follows, therefore, that he
expresses in his work the habits, aspirations, and the
life of the society in which he lives. The habits, aspirations, and the life of a given society, Morris believed,
are based on the economic condition of the people of
that society. The art of any epoch is necessarily the
expression of its social life.[31] Industrial freedom and
the flourishing of art have always gone together; industrial slavery and the degradation of the arts are ac-

[30]Morris, *Art and its Producers*, pp. 22, 23; *Hopes and Fears for Art*, p. 178.
[31]Morris, *Architecture*, etc., pp. 204-05, 215.

companying each other at the present time.   History
demonstrated conclusively to Morris that wherever there
has been hope of progress, the works of art which have
come down from that period show such hope.[32]

The art-remains of the period from 1280 to 1320
proved to Morris the truth of his assertions regarding the relation of art to life.   This was the luxuriant
blossoming time in architecture for all of the races which
had held fast to historical tradition; the loveliest and
the most elevating works of art were produced in these
years.   Moreover, the taste for the beautiful and a
knowledge of how to use it was spread broadly among
the people.   In fact, taste and knowledge were really
instinctive.   The finely-wrought armor of the knights,
the marvelous and intricate decorations in stone and
wood-work in cathedrals, abbeys, and chapels,—and
even in the humblest cottages of the artisans,—the
splendid illumination of the missals, the manner in which
intricate designs and beautiful tracery were applied in
out of the way corners where the eye could never pene-
trate, the loving ornamentation of furniture and the
commonest utensils of daily use, all bear testimony to
the statement that taste and the requisite knowledge
to express it were spread broadly among the people.
Morris sweepingly asserted that no piece of handicraft
was ugly in those days; each one had its inevitable form,
and was profusely and elaborately ornamented according to the taste and invention of the maker.   The great
minsters, the palaces of the nobility, the small grey
churches, the little grey cottages, were all built, Morris
insisted, not by great architects, sitting apart from common men and making designs to be executed by under-
lings who had no part in the aspirations of the master-
artists' souls; but by common men,—the monk, the
the village carpenter, the mason.[33]   Gothic architecture,

[32]Morris, *Architecture*, etc., p. 79.
[33]See Vasari's *Lives of the Painters*.   Morris is wrong in supposing that there
were no great architects in mediaeval times.   He is undoubtedly right in his statement that they were not set apart from the common people who worked out their
plans; they understood one another.   They never had such difficulty as Morris and
Burne-Jones had when they tried to furnish their first rooms.

which to-day fills the minds of men with the noble and exalted thoughts which animated the builders, was wrought by such humble workmen.   To Morris this was evidence that the art of the Middle Ages, like the art of Greece, was loved and cherished, and that the production of art was the spontaneous expression of the ideas of the times.   It is a significant fact that the progressive part of the society of the time, the democratic element, was the most active in the development of art.

Although such boundless praise is given to the mediaeval period as the very blossoming time of art, it may be objected that the conditions of life at that time were far from being delightful.   Under the feudal system the workmen assuredly were often oppressed.   Morris made no denial of this point.   He admitted freely the strong demarcation of classes with all that such demarcation implies; yet he believed that it was a demarcation more artificial than real.[34]   The feudal lords did not extend distinctions of rank to the minds and the imaginations of men; the question was one rather of splendor and non-splendor, of the outward shows of life, not of refinement and vulgarism.   The language, manners, and ideas of the various classes showed no

[34]See Gibbins, DeB. H., *Industry in England*, pp. 172 ff.   Gibbins is in agreement with Thorold Rogers in his account of the peasants' revolt and of the good condition of the laborers immediately following it, although some modern historians have criticized Rogers.   Gibbins insists in his reading of the documents that wages were high for both artisans and laborers, and that many an agricultural laborer in the last decade of the nineteenth century would have been very glad to receive such wages as were paid in the later fourteenth and fifteenth centuries.   This statement does not leave out of account the purchasing power of wages.   Moreover, as was characteristic of the Middle Ages, superior workmen received but little more than those under them; indeed, there was no such enormous difference between the squire and his laborers as there is to-day between employer and employed; nor were there such extremes of poverty and wealth.   Of course the mediaeval period had its drawbacks; there was more hardship, and disease was more fatal, and life more hazardous; but England, Gibbins says, was really a "Merrie England."

It must be remarked, however, that Morris was not explicit as to the time or period when he spoke of the conditions of life in the Middle Ages.   What he said was intended to apply rather generally, and is perhaps too sweeping; but it is nevertheless borne out in the main by several modern historians. (See Gibbins, pp. 172ff., and the authorities whom he cites.)   Morris, because of his temperament and training, was no doubt inclined to minimize the hardships and privations of mediaeval life because he saw in the remains of mediaeval art proof that men had been free and therefore happy in their work, however bound down by authority and restriction in other ways.   It must not be concluded, however, that Morris failed to appreciate the short-comings of the Middle Ages.

such startling differences as at the present time. And
although the crafts were united into guilds, which
guarded rigidly and divided rigidly the occupations of
men, there was little competition in the markets. This
was due to the fact that only the surplus was sold; wares
were made first for domestic consumption. Within the
guilds there was comparatively slight division of labor.
A man understood how to make his wares from the first
process to the end. He felt a great pride and responsibility for the excellence of the finished product. The
piece of work admirably made was the Open Sesame for
the apprentice to the master. Thus the unit of labor
was an intelligent man. He did not need to speed his
work; he could proceed with it in a leisurely manner,
and take thought as he went. According to his capacity
and according to the ideas he had in common with all
the people,—the noblemen included,[35]—so he wrought.
In other words, the workman, whatever his political and
social status, was free in his work. His wares were
made, not for profit first, but for use. Morris's study
of the remains of mediaeval art led him to the conclusion
that no cultivation, no share in the science which is outside and beyond the life of the workman, can supply the
place of freedom of hand and thought in a man's working hours and his interest in the final product of his hand.
The collective genius of a people working in free, harmonious coöperation can produce results of greater
power in the popular arts than a great artist can who
is far in advance, yet out of touch with his workmen.[36]

[35]Morris, *Architecture*, etc., pp. 180-81.
[36]Morris, *Art and its Producers*, pp. 5-8. Cf. Henry Dyer, *The Evolution of Industry*, p. 65: " . . . it cannot be denied that, notwithstanding all the drawbacks
of the system, the Socialists have some ground for speaking of the good old days of
the feudal system with something more than approval, affording as they did opportunities for an open-air, natural life, accompanied, it might be, by few luxuries, but
generally by a rude plenty and by possibilities for art, at least in its social applica-
tions such as are not likely to be found under the system of selfish competition."
See also J. B. Clark, *The Philosophy of Wealth*, p. 175. Where there was the mediaeval system of industrial coöperation, there breathed a spirit of fraternalism, and
"justice, rather than force, presided over the distribution of wealth."
　　Besides the individual freedom accorded the mediaeval worker in his work, the
craft guilds stood for honest goods at honest prices. This, of course, is of great significance, because the performance of good, honest work is promotive of character
in the worker and enjoyment in his work. One cannot forget, however, the oppression of craftsmen by merchants, and of the poorer freemen by the craftsmen
in the latter's years of aristocratic arrogance.

But one change brings about another. Political and economic changes modified gradually the methods of work. The aspirations of the people of five hundred years ago toward freedom and progress were checked by such economic developments as the enclosures, the degeneracy and breaking-down of the guild system, the sudden development of commerce, and the growth of markets. In the latter half of the sixteenth century, the employer and the free workman emerged; men were gathered into shops; tool machinery was improved, until finally division of labor appeared. Division of labor reached a stage in the eighteenth century when the unit of labor was no longer a single workman making an article of utility and beauty from its first process to the finished product; the unit of labor was a group of men, all of the group together working on the article; that is, they took the place of, or acted like a machine. The next stage of advance turned the workman from a machine into a mere tender or operative of a machine.[37] The gradual decline of the arts, both intellectual and decorative, according to Morris, accompanied this industrial development. At first, the romance or soul of the arts withered; and then, as the idea of profit,— the idea of commerce as an end and not as a means of life, gained a hold on the minds of men, the decline went even further. There are still a few goods made by the workshop system, but these workshops are being gradually displaced by the all-pervading factory system, in which human machines become mere accessories to machines.[38]

To modern development, then, Morris charges the death of art. The people no longer have the opportunity to produce art; they no longer understand what it means. The little remnant of art which is left belongs to the class which Morris has designated as great art.

[37]Morris, *Architecture*, etc., p. 219.

[38]*Ibid.*, p. 182. Nevertheless it should be noted that, on the whole, the modern survivals of the guild, the domestic and the workshop economies, are, in many cases, more dangerous to the health and happiness of the worker than is the factory, because in the latter, effective union organization and efficient public regulation are more easily secured than in the modern survivals of the older forms of manufacturing.

But it has no spiritual effect on the people, for they no longer participate in the production of beauty, and therefore they cannot comprehend it, cannot appreciate it.   And the imaginative artists, those who best and most highly express for us the worth and meaning of life, are in their turn hindered and hampered because they are living on alien ground, and because the best work can never be aught but the blossom of all the half-conscious work below it.[39]   The lesser arts under such conditions have become mechanical; they express no intelligence except the intelligence of the designer. Tradition no longer guides the popular arts.   The artist has risen above the handicraftsman; the latter has no hope of rising and no intelligent sympathy with the former.

It is with art [Morris said sadly] as it fares with a company of soldiers before a redoubt, when the captain runs forward full of hope and energy but looks not behind to see if his men are following, and they hold back, not knowing why they are brought to die; the captain's life is spent for nothing, and his men are sullen prisoners in the redoubt of unhappiness and Brutality.[40]

It is evident from Morris's analysis that art bears the closest relation to life, to social conditions.   "Art is the expression of man's joy in his labor"; it is his solace; it is the spiritual element, the soul of labor, some creation of his which appeals to his emotion and to his intellect by means of his senses.   All things, even the humblest, which are made by man should have this soul-element in them, else they will disgrace the fair face of nature. To deprive man of the opportunity of translating his thought into the product of his hands, Morris declared again and again, is to deprive him of happiness, of life, of all that makes a worthy man.

Work well done, it may be repeated by way of summary, under wholesome conditions, is the very foundation stone of Morris's art-doctrine.   Work well done, under wholesale conditions, tends to conserve the race from intellectual death, for it is the prerequisite to all worthy

[39]Morris, *Hopes and Fears for Art*, pp. 77, 79.
[40]*Ibid.*, p. 11.

civilization and progress. Man needs both to create
beauty and to live under the influences of beauty. To
live amid ugliness is to debase both nature and the worker,
is to deprive the worker of happiness. It is not enough
that a few carefully nurtured persons should endeavor
to produce art; their efforts are vain if all the people do
not share in its creation and understanding. To hold
that a few geniuses are ample to supply the beautiful
needed by man, ample to guard the fairness of the earth,
is to admit that the heritage of civilization is for the
few, that progress is for the few, that unhappiness and
degradation are for the many. Fortunately for civilization conditions forbid that the few may have art when
the many are deprived of it. Riches the few may have,
but not beauty; luxury they may have, but not culture.
The beauty spontaneously created by the people is a
positive necessity of worthy life for all; and it is the
standard by which to measure the civilization of all in
any one epoch. The only art which will be a means of
progress to the world, rather than a positive hindrance,
is, in the democratic doctrine of Morris, an art made by
the people, and for the people, as a happiness to the
maker and user.[41]

[41]Morris, *Hopes and Fears for Art*, p. 66.

CHAPTER II

To Morris, with his temperament and mentality, modern civilization presented many and terrible flaws. Toward certain developments of this civilization he was unqualifiedly hostile. The contrast between mediaeval art and the pseudo-art of his day called forth in him a bitter, uncompromising spirit. Nor did he lack opportunities of making frequent, unfavorable comparisons. Evidences of the kind of art he deeply admired, an "art made by the people and for the people as a joy to the maker and user" he found not only all over England, but thickly scattered as well in Continental countries; in the ancient, weathered churches, in the little grey houses, the hoary abbeys, and in the noble magnificence of Gothic cathedrals, which to this day touch the soul with the aspirations once stirring in the hearts of the builders. The scraps of art treasured in museums tell the same story of the happy work-life of mankind. Beauty once "inevitably created by the hand of man" contrasted with ugliness daily created by the machines of man carried to Morris a menace of powerful import to civilization. For ugliness, in his analysis, contains a double curse. Not only is there the curse of ugliness objectified, but also the curse of the influence of ugliness in men's lives. Ugliness carries a spiritual penalty; it kills in the hearts of men even the desire for beauty. The result has been that cultivated persons nowadays often do not take seriously the necessity for art as a part of the actual life of the people; they no longer appreciate that for the proper development of human souls association with beauty is imperative. For the masses the most serious problem of life is the problem of earning the wherewithal to buy mere food, clothing, and shelter. Perhaps some one will retort that always, throughout the history of mankind, have

the people been obliged to struggle for a bare existence.
But Morris would have the world know that although
in ancient and mediaeval times their lives might indeed
have been hard-pressed with poverty, yet in their poverty
the joy had always been theirs of making beautiful things
in perfect freedom of spirit.   But to-day, when they
feel the need of beauty spiritually to enlighten their
lives,—and the word *when* is significant,—they cannot
by any means satisfy that need.   Efforts to still their
feeble desires in this direction lead them to buy cheap
and gaudy ornament,—ornament their ancestors would
have scorned.   But neither can the rich buy things of
such beauty as were made centuries ago by common
people working under conditions which allowed them
freedom to express their thoughts in the products of
their hands.   They who at the present time possess the
earth often do not even care seriously for such art; they
have lost the sense of its spiritual and cultural power.
London itself will furnish an example of the point under
discussion.   It is "the richest city of the richest age of
the world," Morris wrote, "yet every crime against art,
every piece of ugliness, every vulgarity is shared equally
by dwellers of Bethnal Green and the modern palaces
of the West End."[1]   A good illustration, this, of the way
in which people's lives are all bound together, no matter
how keenly they may feel their separateness.   This
double Nemesis Morris charged to the system under
which industry is at present organized.

This stinging indictment of the existing economic
system necessitates a closer inquiry into the state of art
at the present time.   Morris made the simplest of divi-
sions in discussing the point.   Everything made by the
hand of man must either be beautiful or ugly.   Compare
he said, the relics of the art of by-gone epochs,—common wares, household goods used for every day, and
exchanged freely with neighbors,—with the things made
now for the same purposes.   The eye cannot fail to be
struck by the difference.   Money cannot buy in these

[1]Morris, *Hopes and Fears for Art*, pp. 176-77.

times wares such as all might have in the old days. Morris's conclusion has no nuances: Beauty characterizes the art of our fathers; ugliness characterizes the art of our contemporaries.[2]   The answer is so dogmatic that it is certain to arouse the objection that although it may be conceded that things used in daily life are ugly, yet so opprobious a term can hardly be applied to great or intellectual art, the product of those endowed with very special gifts of expressing in their work their dreams and ideals.   Morris of course granted that it is indeed true that the nineteenth century can point to men of rare genius who have carved and painted wonder-works.   These works of high art are, however, produced under almost superhuman difficulties, because, lacking the sympathetic coöperation of a nation of artist-workmen below them, their creators have to work alone.   They lack an atmosphere of art; they are cut off from art tradition,

that wonderful, almost miraculous accumulation of the skill of ages, which men find themselves partakers of without effort on their part.   The knowledge of the past and the sympathy with it which the artists of to-day have, they have acquired, on the contrary, by their own most strenuous individual effort; and as the tradition no longer exists to help them in their practice of the art, and they are heavily weighted in the race by having to learn everything from the beginning, each man for himself, so also, and that is worse, the lack of it deprives them of a sympathetic and appreciative audience.   Apart from the artists themselves and a few persons who would be artists but for want of opportunity and for insufficient gifts of hand and eye, there is in the public of to-day no real knowledge of art and little love of it.[3]

And such works of art are for the rich alone.

Morris's position on these points will be clearer if an examination is made of his analysis of work.   From his knowledge of the past and from his study of the present Morris classified work under three heads: first, mechanical toil; second, intelligent work; third, imaginative work.   By mechanical toil he meant machine work,

[2]Morris, *Architecture*, etc., pp. 83-84.
[3]Morris, *Architecture*, etc., p. 168.

work done by men who put no thought into their productions and could put none if they wished to; for they work under a system which concentrates all effort, not on the quality of the work, not on the excellence of the goods, but on profit alone. By intelligent work Morris meant to connote work which *may* be more or less mechanical, but which can still be done better or worse. In other words, the workman has the opportunity, if he wishes,—and he will always so wish, if he has the chance, Morris believed,—of expressing his individuality in his work. His extra care will be compensated for by the pleasure he finds in the actual doing of his work. By imaginative work Morris meant work wholly individual, work which never could have been done by any other artist or workman. The difference between the second and third kinds is one only of degree. Mechanical toil is the product of a civilization which has for its end the making of profits, instead of "reverence for the life of man on earth." The result of such work as this, Morris asserted, is that it will kill all art, even the highest, if left in undisputed sway. Intelligent work, on the other hand, is born of a progressive civilization full of hope for itself and productive of happiness in the lives of the workers. Imaginative work is the crown of civilization, expressing man's yearning after the ideal; "it bears in its bosom the worth and meaning of life and the counsel to strive to understand everything, to fear nothing and to hate nothing: in a word, 'tis the symbol and the sacrament of the Courage of the world." In our age, as Morris saw it, mechanical toil has devoured intelligent work and even some part of imaginative work, until "the enormous mass of the very worst now confronts a slender but still bright array of the very best; what is left of art is rallied to its citadel of the highest intellectual art, and stands at bay there."[4]

It is abundantly clear that it is with mechanical toil that Morris quarreled. It alone is responsible for the production of ugliness,—an ugliness pregnant with many evil consequences. A discussion of some of these conse-

[4]Morris, *Hopes and Fears for Art*, pp. 207-10.

quences will serve to bring out Morris's view. In addition to depriving men of beauty in the common wares of daily use, in addition to hampering the intellectual artist and depriving him of appreciators, it has done a still further injury to civilization. It has defiled nature. The mere animal cravings of man urge him to turn often to nature for solace in his weariness. And nature ought to be able to respond. It ought to be beautiful and fair even where man dwells and has his busiest marts. Its air should be pure, its rivers clear, its trees unmaimed and undestroyed.

Not only [said Morris passionately] are London and our great commercial cities mere masses of sordidness, filth, and squalor, embroidered with patches of pompous and vulgar hideousness, no less revolting to the eye and the mind when one knows what it means; not only have whole counties of England and the heavens that hang over them disappeared under a crust of unutterable grime, but the disease, which, to a visitor coming from the times of art, reason and order,[5] would seem to be a love of dirt and ugliness for its own sake, spreads all over the country, and every little market town seizes the opportunity to imitate, as far as it can, the majesty of the hell of London and of Manchester. . . . Not only are the cities a disgrace to us, and the smaller towns a laughing stock; not only are the dwellings of man grown inexpressibly base and ugly, but the very cowsheds and cart-stables, nay, the merest piece of farm engineering are tarred with the same brush. Even if a tree is cut down or blown away, a worse one, if any, is planted in its stead, and, in short, our civilization is passing like a blight, daily growing heavier and more poisonous, over the whole face of the country, so that every change is sure to be a change for the worse in its outward aspect. So then it comes to this, that not only are the minds of great artists narrowed and their sympathies frozen by their isolation, not only has co-operative art come to a standstill, but the very food on which both the greater and lesser arts subsist is being destroyed; the well of art is poisoned at its spring.[6]

But man does not stop with the mutilation of nature; he makes the earth still more hideous by the way in which

[5]Morris is here carried away by his enthusiasm. Undoubtedly the crowded condition of modern towns, cities, and factory industries, and the greater activity of modern life have increased the necessity for sanitary regulation; yet evidence is not lacking to show that the Middle Ages were not without their insanitary conditions. D. H. Montgomery, *The Leading Facts of English History*, pp. 148, 228; H. DeB. Gibbins, *Industry in England*, p. 152; Denton, *Fifteenth Century*, p. 103.
[6]Morris, *Architecture*, etc., pp. 172-3.

he builds.   In spite of the well-meant efforts of design-
ers, many of whom conscientiously strive for beauty
and better architecture, Morris was certain that the
situation was growing worse instead of better; "it is a
matter of course that almost every new house shall be
quite disgracefully and degradingly ugly."[7]   Even the
rich, who have every means of owning decent, beautiful
dwellings and can choose sites which still have some of
the natural beauty of the earth left them, do not seem
to be able to build beautifully.   Their houses, Morris
said emphatically, "are simply blackguardly.   All they
express is hypocrisy, flunkeyism, and careless selfishness."[8]   In a word, they are expressive only of the
worst sides of men's characters.   And yet Morris was
sure that if people could be induced to destroy all of the
ugly buildings which have been erected in the modern
period, and should build others to take their places, the
new architecture would be quite as bad as the old; some
of the buildings would be even more vulgar in sham and
meaningless ornament than those there are at present.
Of course houses designed by artists of imagination and
skill would naturally escape this condemnation; but at
their best they could not equal the ordinary little church,
the ordinary little house built five hundred years ago.
It is the oft-reiterated reason which Morris gives for
this: however eager they may be to produce beauty and
art, artists now have no living tradition to aid them in
their work; they can only imitate.   And yet imitation
is not successful because the mason, the carpenter, the
joiner, the carver have each to be taught to imitate also;
they have lost the gift of their fathers to produce beauty
unconsciously, by instinct.[9]

Uncompromising as was Morris's denunciation of the
state of art in the present epoch, he did not entirely forget that there are some refined people who really love
art and are willing to make considerable sacrifices to get
it; and that there is, in consequence, a small band of

7*Ibid.*, p. 86.
8Morris, *Hopes and Fears for Art*, p. 121.
9Morris, *Art and its Producers*, pp. 31-33.

artists who possess to a very high degree the power of fine execution, together with imagination and a good intellect, who are working hard to do something for the regeneration of the lesser arts.   He recognized also that altogether they have accomplished an appreciable amount, although their efforts have not met with such great success as they deserve.

Morris was not content with laying all the blame for the great blight on art on mechanical toil alone.   He was not satisfied until he went back even of the *why*. Who, in the last analysis, is the enemy responsible for taking the meaning out of life?   Morris found the answer to be Luxury,—Luxury, whose parent is Riches, not Wealth; Luxury, a child of the age of commerce, the enslaver not only of the poor man toiling under grinding misery to make more riches, but also of the foolish and not altogether happy man who must buy what the toiler produces.   Luxury shows its face where art was wont to dwell; it is the changeling of art.   Its companions are effeminacy and brutality, destroyers of the self-respect of all classes.[10]   Those who think that the difference between barbarism and civilization lies in the greater number of comforts which the latter can bestow merely serve to prove how vulgar and degraded have become the people of the present.

I had thought [wrote Morris] that civilization meant the attainment of peace and order and freedom, of good-will between man and man, of the love of truth, and the hatred of injustice, and by consequence, the attainment of the good life which these things breed, a life free from craven fear, but full of incident; that was what I thought it meant, not more stuffed chairs and more cushions, and more carpets and gas and more dainty meat and drink— and therewithal more and sharper differences between class and class.[11]

It will be noted that Morris said that riches is the parent of luxury.   Riches he distinguished from wealth. He saw a real difference between them.   Wealth to him connoted the means of living a decent life.   In his analysis it is of two kinds: first, food, clothing, and

[10]Morris, *Architecture*, etc., pp. 100-11.
[11]Morris, *Hopes and Fears for Art*, p. 107.

shelter, or those things which pertain to the body; and second, art and knowledge, or those things which pertain to the mind. Riches, in Morris's definition, are the means of exercising dominion over others.[12]

> Wealth is what Nature gives us, and what a reasonable man can make out of the gifts of Nature for his reasonable use. The sunlight, the fresh air, the unspoiled face of the earth, food, raiment, and housing necessary and decent; the storing up of knowledge of all kinds, and the power of disseminating it; means of free communication between man and man; works of art, the beauty which man creates when he is most a man, most aspiring and thoughtful, —all things which serve the people, free, manly, and uncorrupted, —this is wealth.[13]

And art has always gone hand in hand with wealth, using the word as Morris defined it.

The capitalistic system Morris held responsible for the destruction of wealth,—both kinds of wealth, bodily and mental. It has indeed created vast riches, and thus vast dominion over man. But it has also created poverty; the two go hand in hand. The rich must have some one to work for them. Riches and poverty, according to Morris's reasoning, connote masters and slaves. That wealth is not the ideal of mankind is proved by what happens whenever a question of profit is raised. Natural beauty is destroyed with never a thought of what is being done; Gothic cathedrals are barbarously restored; perhaps some marvelously beautiful building is pulled down outright to make way for something that will bring profit. The people are robbed of their commons for profit. Railways despoil a fair landscape for profit. Some parts of the country are actually buried in squalor and utter wretchedness for profit.[14] The noble meaning of wealth has been forgotten in the mad pursuit of riches.

A repetition of Morris's explanation of modern industrial organization will serve to make his ideas clearer as to the deeper cause of this gloomy condition. The

[12]Morris, *Architecture*, etc., pp. 80-81.
[13]Morris, *Signs of Change*, p. 149.
[14]Morris, *Architecture*, etc., pp. 97-99.

workers are gathered into immense factories where they are but parts of a machine, or operatives of machines. The army-like organization of modern industry subordinates and very often completely effaces the individual. Labor is divided and subdivided almost infinitely; each worker has only a minute part in the process of making even a comparatively simple article. He depends upon a host of other workers about him; and so on down to the last worker who puts on a product the finishing touch. And this small part in the production of a ware, perhaps by means of operating a certain machine invented for a very small process, he performs all his life. Naturally he is not the most important factor as an individual in the making of the goods; neither are all of the huge army of workers together considered to be the most important factor. The foreman is thought to be of more significance than all of them; and above him are still more and greater personages,—the manager and the capitalist.[15] The workman under such a system cannot, as a rule, nor is he allowed, to put his individuality into his work; he has but one small task to do, and the more mechanically he does it, that is, the less thought he needs to put into the performing of it, by just so much is he considered the better workman, and by just so much the cheaper can the goods be produced.[16]

[15]Morris, *Architecture*, etc., pp. 89-90. A certain well-known economist, when asked how he liked his work at Washington, by way of explanation said that it was worse than State work because one was, in his particular federal employment, only a cog in a very big machine.

[16]Morris, *Architecture*, etc., p. 90. See T. N. Carver, *Machinery and the Laborer*, in *Quarterly Journal of Economics*, 22: 210 ff. In this connection it may be interesting to note that Professor Carver considers it an advantage for workers to be operatives of machines instead of craftsmen doing a whole piece of work from beginning to end. He contends that the old-fashioned shoemaker, for example, was mainly occupied with operations which were, for the most part, merely mechanical. The fact that he was obliged to use many of these operations in making a pair of shoes. required of him, says Professor Carver, great concentration of mind. The modern operative, a tender of a machine, has but one thing to do, and practice makes his work in many cases entirely automatic. Professor Carver expresses the opinion that the modern operative has an advantage over the old-fashioned shoemaker in that he has more opportunity in the performance of his mechanical task for free mental activity, and this because he need not concentrate so strenuously. The question may well be asked, however, whether the modern machine operator has a mind stored by education and travel and contact with men which the leisure of performing a simple automatic operation gives him an opportunity to exercise. Another factor worthy of notice is that the old shoemaker was his own master; if he wished to talk hours with a customer, there was no one to stop him. If he wished

Morris had still a further quarrel with modern times and its organization of industry. The consumer, he declared, has no choice in the matter of what he must buy; he cannot go to his neighbor and say to him: "I should like to have a chair for my living-room; I know that you understand just what I need, and that you will

to take a week or a month of holiday, no one could say him nay. In other words, he was free to indulge the mood of idleness. Further, he could make and follow his own designs and put as much invention into them as the shoe and the customer would allow.

Professor Carver says also that the machine worker appears to have less dehumanizing work than the hand-worker; first, because the machine does the most mechanical and the least human parts, leaving only the less mechanical and the more human parts to be done by men; and second, because the mere contemplation of an efficient and intricate machine at work is a source of mental training to any mind capable of understanding it. In reply let it be said that it is quite evident in this age of machine-made goods that the less mechanical and more human parts of an article are necessarily limited. Large numbers of workmen must therefore be dehumanized by doing dehumanizing work, since only a few can do the more human parts. As to the second reason given by Professor Carver for the superiority of machine-work, although it is true that the working of a complex or intricate machine may be interesting, and may even inspire an inventively-inclined operative to make improvements on it, yet it must be admitted that to watch a machine operating from eight to ten hours a day, for six days a week for forty or more years, even if occasional inventions are added to it, must certainly fail to make up to the workman what he loses by never having had the opportunity to work out a single design of the aricle for which perhaps he is making the hundreth part, by never having had the pleasure of adding anything of his own thought to it in its execution, by never having had any *variety* in his work, any conception of giving pleasure to anyone else because he has made a piece of art as excellent as he could make it. In other words, Professor Carver takes no account of the spiritual power of doing good work. The very things which he finds to criticize about the hand-worker's life are the very things which make a real man of him, which develop his faculties and his soul. Undoubtedly the money cost of production of any given article, for example, shoes, is lowered for both the capitalist and the consumer under the system of the division of labor and machine-made goods; but Morris is certainly right when he insists that the cost of production is not lowered for society by such work. He even goes further and says that the cost of production is raised for society because what the producer loses of spiritual development, cultural power, and pleasure in his work far overbalances what the consumer and capitalist save in mere money-cost. It should not be inferred from the foregoing discussion of Professor Carver's points that the use of machines in the production of goods is an unmixed evil in the opinion of the writer. Most people agree with Morris in his belief that all unattractive or merely mechanical work should be done by machinery; indeed, that many more machines ought to be used for such work than is the case at present. Morris contends that thereby the worker could be freed at least to some extent for work on a whole article with his hands. With some such freedom, a conception of what good work really means would come to the producer; and he would realize, as did the craftsmen of mediaeval days, that the user or consumer, who was most often a neighbor of the producer, had definite wants to be satisfied and definite ideas as to what the thing should be which was to supply his wants. He would be conscious of making the article for a man of like needs with himself; he would understand human necessities; and the wares he fashioned, so constructed, so understood, would be works of art, and just what the consumer wished. See Morris, *Art and its Producers*, pp. 4-5.

make it exactly as if you were going to have it in your own house." The user, like the worker, has become a slave to the world-market,[17] a man with a purse in his pocket; yet he cannot dictate what he wants to the man behind the counter; he has rather to take what he can get to supply his wants. Morris put the condition of the consumer too strongly perhaps; yet the buyer, except so far as competition and the law of monopoly take account of his wishes, must accept the dictation, to a very considerable extent, of the manufacturer, who too often manages to cultivate in the consumer false wants. But Morris is right in his general statement that the market does not conform to man, but man to the market. Over and over again he insisted that the laborer does not and need not feel any responsibility in the production of an article of utility; he is a dependent, and can think only of earning a livelihood for himself and for his family.[18] Neither is the consumer often in a position to protest effectually. The captain of industry thinks neither of the workman, nor of the buyer, nor does he often think even of the quality of the wares; but only that there is a certain demand for a certain utility; or, perhaps, the possibility of developing a certain demand in the world-market which it is his opportunity to supply as cheaply as possible in such a way that he make the highest profit. To be sure, the fact that there is a demand for a certain kind of goods means that the manufacturer must govern his operations with some reference to this demand. He must come up to a certain standard in the goods, or *seem* to come up to it, else the public will revolt outright. To Morris the result of such a system is obvious. Goods resembling outwardly at least what may be called the real thing are made—commercial shams, makeshifts, for the most part they are. By putting these on the market at a low price, the manufacturer coerces the public into purchasing his goods. One effect of the present practice is that not only does the consumer not get real goods, but real goods cease to be made after

[17]Morris, *Art and its Producers*, p. 12.
[18]Morris, *Art and its Producers*, p. 35.

shams and makeshifts have been successfully launched upon the market.[19]

To the commercial producer the actual wares are nothing; their adventures in the market are everything.[20]   To the artist the wares are everything; his market he need not trouble himself about; for he is asked by other artists to do what he does; what his capacity urges him to do.

The ethics of the commercial person (squaring themselves of course to his necessities) bid him give as little as he can to the public; and take as much as he possibly can from them; the ethics of the artist bid him put as much of himself as he can into every piece of goods he makes.   The commercial person, therefore, is in this position: that he is dealing with a public of enemies; the artist, on the contrary, with a public of friends and neighbors.[21]

"Society," Morris said on another occasion, "is based on a state of perpetual war."[22]   This war is competition. Many people, including some economists, have said that competition is a desirable thing, conducive to progress, —nay, that it is a necessary concomitant of progress. But is war an inevitable means of progress?   War, said Morris, involves the pursuit of selfish ends,—gain at the loss of some one else, and not much care as to how that gain is made; not much care as to how much waste and destruction accompanies it.

This state of constant commercial warfare is manifested in several ways.   First, in Morris's analysis, there is that form of war called national rivalry.   History admits that all modern wars have been mostly commercial.   When a nation has the lion's share of the world-market for its products, as was the case with England in the nineteenth century, it is obviously not necessary to make war on other nations to seize it from them.   But as soon as there is the slightest danger of losing an important market to another nation, cannons are cleaned and gun-powder is manufactured in preparation to ruin the obnoxious rival.   Not only is war

[19]Morris, *Art and its Producers*, pp. 35-36.
[20]The writer would add, too, that very often in this age the aim of those in control of a business is not commercial or industrial, but financial; they manage the business primarily to make money out of operations in its stocks and bonds.
[21]Morris, *Art and its Producers*, pp. 38-39.
[22]Morris, *Signs of Change*, p. 4.

made on civilized nations, but also on savage tribes.
Many times these are ruthlessly conquered, not primarily
to bring them into the fold of the blessed, as the pious
women of missionary societies suppose, not to civilize
them in the best sense, as many not uneducated and
well-informed people think, but merely to open a new
market.[23]   But not only is there war between civilized
nations, and war between civilized nations and bar-
barians, but great capitalists, great firms war among
themselves; or, in the language of political economy,
they compete with each other for the opportunity to
sell their products.   A market, for example, demands
certain goods.   All of the manufacturers of these goods
speedily set to work to supply this demand, each trying
to the utmost to produce the cheapest in order to get
as much of the market as possible.   Adulteration and
tricks, as is well-known, play a large part in their efforts
to put goods on the market at lower prices than other
manufacturers, or to reap large profits.   What is the
effect, what *must* be the effect of so many manufacturers
all competing, all warring with each other for the opportunity to supply the market?   Besides the cheapness and the nastiness of the wares, naturally there will
be an over-supply; prices will sink; waste and misery
all around are the inevitable results.   The cheapness
of the article is purchased in the end at a heavy price;
therefore its cheapness is only apparent, not real.   The
consumer is cheated in the wares he purchases; the
laborer is starved, for presently the factory is shut
down because of the glut in the market.   The only ones
who gain anything by this sudden eddy in the stream
of commerce are the manufacturers.   Morris frankly
called them gamblers.[24]
     What is the effect on the workers of all this national
and capitalistic rivalry?   The workers, as has been
noted, are trained to do one sort of task.   This task is
usually only a small part in the production of any one
article; this is their life-work.   It has been shown how

[23]Morris, *Signs of Change*, pp. 6-7.
[24]Morris, *Signs of Change*, pp. 10-11.

the market becomes glutted by the competition of manufacturers among themselves for as large a share of the
market as they can get.   When the over-supply becomes apparent, the factory is shut down.   Usually the
capitalist feels no responsibility for his men.   While
the worker was employed in the factory, he had to go
on feverishly producing goods as if the demand for the
article which he was busily making, with every nerve
strained and every muscle tense in his effort to make
haste, would be eternal.   Persons who ask why the
worker does not work less intensively or shorter hours
when he knows that over-supply is certain, only show
their ignorance of the organization of industry.   But
to return to the tale of supplying a demand. The market
is glutted; the factory is closed.   What can the worker
do now that he is thrown out of employment, now that
he no longer has the opportunity to do the only work
he knows how to do under the present system?   There
is but one answer.   He takes his place among a host
of starvelings until another demand comes for his labor.
He takes his place in the reserve army of labor.   The
existence of the residuum or reserve army is one of the
most serious of the indictments against modern industry.
"If civilization is to go no further than this, it had better
not have gone so far," Morris declared;

if it does not aim at getting rid of this misery and giving some share
in the happiness and dignity of life to *all* the people that it has
created, and which it spends such unwearying energy in creating,
it is simply an unorganized injustice, a mere instrument for oppression, so much the worse than that which has gone before it, as
its pretentions are higher, its slavery subtler, and its mastery harder
to overthrow because supported by such a dense mass of common-
place well-being and comfort.[25]

The existence of this reserve army of labor Morris thought
to be a necessity of the present industrial organization,
an organization based wholly on force.   The employers
war with one another for markets (except where monopo-

---

[25]Morris, *Hopes and Fears for Art*, p. 92.   Morris called the reserve army
not only the unfortunate army, but the *terrible* army; and declared unqualifiedly
that it is necessary to industry as organized.   A better organization of industry in
the labor market would do much, however, to obviate this condition.

ly or trade agreement come into the industrial equation, Morris should have added); the workers war with one another for the wherewithal to buy food, clothing, and shelter except where they are efficiently organized; and since the supply of unskilled labor is practically unlimited, and since the invention of machinery still goes on, and women and children can be used to operate them, that supply of unskilled labor almost always exceeds the demand. People undersell one another in their desire to get work. The capitalists do not have to compel the workers to their tasks; fear of death by starvation is an effectual enough weapon. When so many strive for the mere privilege of working, is it any wonder that the price of labor is kept as low as possible?

Morris carried his analysis of capitalistic production further. Two elements are necessary to the production of wealth: labor and raw material. In our society a comparatively few people have the raw material in their hands; a much greater number are eager to apply labor to the raw material in order that they may be able by their labor to purchase a livelihood. They must therefore compete with one another for the privilege of doing so since there are vast numbers to do work and not enough work to go around. The capitalists, on the other hand, in order that they may live without such labor as the workers do, or manual labor, must exact a profit over and above what it costs them to pay the laborers. Since there are many laborers eager to work, the capitalists, according to Morris, pay them just what it costs to keep them alive and to multiply their kind.[26] The remainder of the value which labor has added to raw material is the profit of the capitalist. The workers, in spite of their sharp competition with one another, try from time to time to raise their pitiable standard of life by means of strikes and other forms of class war. Occasionally they have been able to wrest

[26]The subsistence theory of wages has its value, but only, it might be argued, as pointing out the very lowest limit of wages. A more serviceable limit is standard of living, marking an inferior limit; whereas the productivity of labor, a factor not of precise determination, however, marks the superior limit.

some concessions from their employers; but their success, said Morris, is not often so real as they suppose.

The tribute which the capitalist exacts from the worker by taking everything above the subsistence wage is not merely a precarious living for himself and his, such as the workers are able to earn by their long hours of arduous toil, but such a living as brings to him and to his family all the enjoyments and advantages of civilization,[27] and often such vast power that justice and laws can scarcely reach him.[28] Economic advantage, in the opinion of Morris, certainly lies with the capitalist. Even if he had a great desire to be humane,—and it is certainly true that many capitalists are,—the competitive organization of industry, Morris believed, would not allow him to do so. For if he paid much higher wages than other manufacturers, he could not compete successfully with them; and he would, therefore, soon be out of business altogether.[29] The capitalist, it follows, is as much a part of the system as is the laborer, and is driven by the momentum of the system to act as he does.

Upon closer inspection of the effect upon the lives of the workers of a system based on force, it will be seen that, despite the fact that the laborers are the sole producers of riches according to the belief of Morris,[30] they

[27]"The argument seems conclusive that the general results of inventions of machinery have been more to the advantage of the capitalist than of the laboring class, especially if we include only wage earners in the latter class" (Professor T. N. Carver, *Journal of Economics*, 22:224).—"Auch die unteren Klasses der Gegenwart sind die Kinder eines reichen und einer ganzen grossartigen Jahrhunderts; aber schliesst die Möglichkeit aus, dass sie die Stiefkinder im Haus sind?" asked Professor Schmoller in his famous reply to the attack of von Treitsche." G. Schmoller, *Grundfragen der Socialpolitik und der Volkswirtschaftslehre*, p. 177.

[28]Morris, *True and False Society*, pp. 7-8.

[29]*Ibid.*, p. 11.

[30]Morris accepted the Marxian theory of labor as the explanation of value, and the theory that over and above the subsistence wage that he receives, the worker produces for the benefit of the capitalist a surplus value. "A use-value or useful article," said Marx, "has value only because human labor in the abstract has been embodied or materialized in it" (*Capital*, p. 5). By labor, in his explanation of value, Marx meant socially necessary labor, which he defined as "that required to produce an article under the normal conditions of production, and with the average degree of skill and intensity prevalent at the time"; and further on, he said, "that which determines the magnitude of the value of any article is the amount of labor . . . or labor-time socially necessary for its production" (*Capital*, p. 6). By "socially necessary" Marx evidently meant under given social conditions (*Capital*,

do not live as well as non-producers. That they occupy
an inferior position none will venture to deny. Do we
not openly call them the "lower" classes? Is not their
standard of living almost infinitely inferior? To begin
with material things, the food which they eat and the

p. 167). "The value of a commodity . . . is determined by the quantity of labor
contained in it, but this quantity is itself limited by social conditions. If the time
socially necessary for the production of any commodity alters—and a given weight
of cotton represents, after a bad harvest, more labor than after a good one—all
previously existing commodities of the same class are affected, . . . and their value
at any given time is measured by the labor socially necessary, i.e., by the labor
necessary for their production under the then existing social conditions" (*Capital*,
p. 193). "Nothing can have value without being the object of utility. If a thing
is useless, so is the labor contained in it; the labor does not count as labor, and therefore creates no value" (*Capital*, p. 8). Exchange value he defined as "a definite
social manner of expressing the amount of labor bestowed upon an object" (*Capital*,
p. 54). By labor-power or capacity "is to be understood the aggregate of those
mental and physical capabilities existing in a human being, which he exercises
whenever he produces a use-value of any description" (*Capital*, p. 145). While he
recognized mental labor and even labor of superintendence and management as
value-creating labor, Marx evidently refused to ascribe to the capitalist any indispensable entrepreneur functions. To the capitalist's exclamation: "Have I not
performed the labor of superintendence and of over-looking the spinner? And does
not this labor too create value?" Marx said: "His overlooker and his manager try
to hide their smiles" (*Capital*, p. 174). Nevertheless Marx pointed out that "A
certain stage of capitalist production necessitates that the capitalist be able to devote the whole of the time during which he functions as a capitalist, i.e., as personi-
fied capital, to the appropriation and therefore control of the labor of others, and
to the selling of the products of this labor" (*Capital*, p. 295). From this it may
fairly be concluded that Marx had no appreciation of the value-producing character
—even though much of modern marketing involves waste and graft—of the marketing of goods, nor of the entrepreneur functions that the capitalist often exercises.
Marx's indictment of the capitalist would be more convincing if he had analyzed
thoroughly the productive process, giving full credit for the entrepreneur functions
of the capitalist, who is something more than a mere owner of capital; and had then
emphasized the wastes and frauds of modern production in addition to the altogether too frequent exploitation of labor.

Marx's theory of surplus value rests upon his theory that values are determined
by units of labor-power time absorbed in their creation. Following Marx, assume
that six hours labor-power is worth three shillings, which some assume is the amount
necessary to maintain the worker according to the civilization of his age, and to
enable him to rear and educate children to take his place in the field of labor. Assume a Twelve Hour day (*Capital*, pp. 150-51). Assume a product of ten pounds of
yarn, in which are embodied cotton and wear on the spindle representing two days
of labor of twelve hours each, and six hours labor of spinning. Six hours of labor
produce a value of three shillings, as indicated. The ten pounds of cotton are
worth thirty hours of labor, or fifteen shillings. If the capitalist pays the spinner
three shillings for his six hours of spinning of ten pounds of yarn, there will be no
profit, no surplus value. By compelling the spinner to work, however, twelve hours
for his subsistence wage of three shillings, the capitalist can make a surplus value
of three shillings. In twelve hours the spinner will turn out twenty pounds of
yarn. The cost of cotton and the wear on the spindle will be the value of four days'
labor or twenty-four shillings, which plus three shillings wages for the spinner, will
make a total cost of twenty-seven shillings. In the twenty pounds of yarn are
embodied five days' labor worth six shillings a day, or thirty shillings. Behold a
surplus value of three shillings (*Capital*, pp. 171-80).

clothes which they wear are not so good as those of the upper classes.   This general statement is applicable to the whole working class.   But it is further true that some of them are so ill-fed that they die of slow starvation; whereas others, when trade is dull, when there has been an over-supply in the goods which their particular factory turns out, actually die of quick starvation. Amidst plenty which they cannot pay for, they perish. Of their clothing, the old proverb, "Dirt and grease are the poor man's apparel," tells the sad truth.[31]   The houses in which they are obliged to live are often not fit for men.   Not only are their houses too small for the number of people who must live in them, but the streets and alleys in which their poor homes are located are often horribly over-crowded.   They cannot even have the privilege of lessening the misery of living in wretched squalor, by stepping out into fair gardens or wide, beautiful streets.

Not only did Morris find a contrast in the material conditions of laborers and capitalists; he found a contrast also in the education which each class receives. A workman who can read French or German, unless it is his native language, and who knows anything about the history of the world or of evolution, or has a taste for literature, is a decided exception.[32]   The mediaeval system, while it made sharp distinctions between the classes, did not enforce the distinction now seen between what is understood by the names, the *cultivated* and the *ignorant*.   The difference in the old days was arbitary; the difference in the present epoch is real.   Now "gentle-

---

[31]Morris, *Monopoly*, etc., pp. 3-4.

[32]It is both right and expedient that the worker should have some share in the culture of his time.   It is only just to the worker and it is certainly essential to the necessary social adjustment and to democratic progress especially through equal opportunity.   That the German working classes feel this to be true is indicated by their conscious effort to share in German culture through night schools and lectures provided by their own organizations.   See W. H. Dawson, *Evolution of Modern Germany*, pp. 158-63.   A somewhat similar attitude is shown by the following: "Our movement in advocating industrial education protests most emphatically against the elimination from our public school system of any line of learning now taught.   Education, technically or industrially, must be supplementary to and in connection with our modern school system.   That for which our movement stands will tend to make better workers of our future citizens, better citizens of our future workers."—*Industrial Education*, Published by the American Federation of Labor, Washington, 1910, p. 6.

men and non-gentlemen divide the world."[33]   The
distinction even goes so far that one might almost say
that there are two languages spoken in England: gentle-
men's English and workmen's English.

Two peoples living street by street and door by door, people of
the same blood, and same tongue and at least nominally living
under the same laws, but one civilized and the other uncivilized.
I do not care who gainsays it, I say that this is barbarous and
dangerous; and it goes step by step with the lack of art which the
same classes are forced into; it is a token, in short, of that vulgarity,
to use a hateful word, which was not in existence before modern
times and the blossoming of Competitive Commerce. . . . It is
the result of the system that has trampled down art, and exalted
Commerce into a sacred religion; and it would seem ready, with
the ghastly stupidity which is its principal characteristic, to mock
the Roman satirist for his noble warning by taking it in inverse
meaning, and now bids us all for the sake of life to destroy the
reasons for living.[34]

Still another contrast between the workers and those
above them Morris laid at the door of Competitive
Commerce.   In *Under an Elm-Tree, or, Thoughts in the
Country-Side*, he compared the beauty of animal and
bird life with the ugliness of human beings.

Also the same day I saw some other animals, male and female.
. . . And these animals, both male and female, were ungraceful,
unbeautiful, for they were hay-makers.   Then I bethought me
that as I had seen starlings in Hertfordshire that were of the same
race as the Thames-side starlings, so I had seen or heard of feather-
less two-legged animals of the same race as the thirsty creatures in
the hay-field; they had been sculptured in the frieze of the Parthe-
non, painted on the ceiling of the Sistine Chapel, imagined in literature as the heroes and heroines of romance; nay, when people
had created in their minds a god of the universe, Creator of all that
was, is, or shall be, they were driven to represent him as one of that
same race to which the thirsty hay-makers belonged; as though
supreme intelligence and the greatest measure of grace and beauty
and majesty were at their highest in the race of those ungainly
animals. . . . The hay-field is a pretty sight under the elm . . .
till you look at the hay-makers closely.[35]

In material comforts and even necessities, in education
and in culture, in beauty of form and face, and in leisure

[33]Morris, *Architecture*, etc., p. 93.
[34]Morris, *Architecture*, etc., p. 107.
[35]Morris, *Under an Elm-Tree*, etc., pp. 7-8.

and holidays there are marked differences between the workers and those who live by their toil.

Altogether, no one can deny that the working class is in an inferior and degraded position. Nor are there many who will say that misery and degradation are the divinely ordered accompaniments of labor. The law of nature indeed demands that all men should labor in order to live; but that law seems to be reversed since those who work most toilsomely get the least compensation, and those who work the least, get the most. Morris saw in all this simply the result of a system based on force.[36]

To the competitive system Morris also charged the clearly marked and rather fixed division of people into classes. Ever since man discovered that he could produce more than he needed for his subsistence, instead of killing the captives conquered in war, he made slaves of them, and commanded them to work, thus gaining profits for himself. In the division of classes in our own age Morris named: first, the aristocracy, who do not pretend to work; second, the middle-classes, some of whom really work hard, but have their labor lightened by leisure and variety; third, the working-classes, who do nothing but work, and have the most inferior and degraded position of the three, "worse off than the beasts of the field."[37] Their only hope is that they may by thrift rise into the class above them. This is, however, often but a phantom hope.[38]

Naturally, with his point of view, Morris had nothing to say in complimentary vein of the production and the consumption of the two higher classes. His discussion of the matter is worth summarizing. The fact that the rich do not work does not prevent them from consuming a great deal; in Morris's estimation they are mere burdens on the community since they live off the two classes below them.[39] The middle-classes, Morris grudgingly

[36]Morris, *Monopoly*, etc., p. 12.
[37]Morris, *Signs of Change*, p. 145.
[38]Morris, *Monopoly*, etc., p. 7.
[39]Morris would undoubtedly have acknowledged that the American rich who produce commercial and industrial utilities are very useful to society; but it might be ventured that his condemnation would be most severe of those whose business

admitted, do work pretty hard, but they do not produce in the same way that the workers do; and, moreover, they consume more than their share.   Those who work in the distribution of goods, produce wastefully. Morris granted that physicians, artists, and literary men are genuine producers; but he was of the opinion that they also consume more than their production justifies. The commercial and manufacturing portion of the middle-classes, those who are most powerful, war or compete among themselves for their share of wealth which they, as a class, take by force from the workers, that is, from those of the middle-classes who are engaged in genuine production as distinguished from distributing and merchandizing.   These latter work, for the most part, for the upper classes; "they are parasites of property, sometimes as in the case of lawyers, undisguisedly so, sometimes, as in the case of the physicians and others above mentioned, professing to be useful, but too often of no use, save as supports of the system of folly, fraud, and tyranny of which they form a part."[40]   The aim of the whole class is not to produce utilities, but to gain such a position either for themselves or for their posterity that they may not have to work.   The third class, the workers, support the upper classes; yet in spite of this fact, they are themselves degraded in both body and mind.   But even some of this class do not produce usefully; they are parasites of property, as for example, soldiers and sailors who work in the interests of national rivalries.   Along with the latter, Morris, who, it is clear, held to the old distinction between so-called productive and unproductive labor, classed the domestic servants, clerks, and shop-assistants employed by the middle classes.[41]

But in spite of the heavy toil of the workers, upon whom rests, it may truly be said, the burden of the world,

activity may be described as consisting of financial jockeying and exploitation as contrasted with production.

[40]Morris, *Signs of Change*, pp. 146-47.

[41]It is curious to note in this connection that, except in a very general way, Morris has nowhere accused the woman of property of being a parasite rather than so accusing her servant. It is certainly more logical to fasten the term *parasite* to the woman of property or of other income who does not, by a reasonable standard, justify her existence, than to the woman's servant, who does the woman's work.

not wealth alone results, but also waste. This is one of Morris's most passionate quarrels with the modern system. If all the terrible moiling in the treadmill of industry could be shown to serve eventually some worthy end, however small, even though the distribution of the goods were faulty and unjust, Morris could perhaps have condoned it. But he was firm in the belief that no such claim could be made. Goods intended to be useful he saw plastered with sham ornament only to be made more ugly and vulgar. They lack all signs of humanity, of intelligence. Ornament made by a machine operated by a man working like a machine can but result in ugliness, for the labor that made it was unpleasurable and oppressive. Bad enough when weary hands and lifeless brains make something intended to be of use, something really necessary in carrying on the business of the world! But how terrible when souls are deadened and happiness strangled to make Nothing! Not only Nothing, but worse than Nothing! For some things with which people clutter their lives are positive hindrances to the greatest efficiency of thought and pleasure. Think of a perfect army engaged in making Nothing, and worse than Nothing! Any person who goes into a Christmas bazaar or a five-and-ten-cent store may without further effort prove for himself the truth of Morris's accusation. The horrors in birch bark, in tinsel, in celluloid, and in aluminum everywhere stare him in the face, and finally almost force him to sell his soul to meet conventional obligations. Toilers to make the wares, machinists to make the machines to make the wares, clerks to sell the wares, and finally people to buy the wares! No wonder Morris felt the situation to be all but hopeless. Then add to the useless and to the worse than useless goods, adulterated foods and drinks, and few will condemn Morris for his vehemence in denouncing the waste of the present industrial system.[42] Then consider the worker

[42]Morris, *Architecture*, etc., pp. 84-112. The Massachusetts Commission (1910) on the High Cost of Living states in its report (p. 338): "It has been estimated that $100,000,000 worth of fraudulently prepared food is consumed in the United States each year. About 90% of this is officially classified as not prejudicial to health;

further as a part of the public, as one who has to buy
the cheap, vulgar, and meaningless goods he has had
to produce under unhappy circumstances. He must
labor without natural solace or joy at the making of
poison, and then he has to buy what he and his fellows
have made.   And in all of the ceaseless round, no one
and nothing have been considered except profit.   Only
the worst, Morris declared, can be expected from such
an epoch.   Things may look very peaceful from the
outside, and people may talk glibly and optimistically
of the blessings of civilization, including those of international transportation and communication; but
Morris refused to see any meaning in such so-called
blessings so long as an enormous number of human
beings are denied life and joy all for the making of a
heap of rubbish, and the taste of the people is such that
the rubbish is marketable.   So great is the need of employment that none may refuse to work; and so cunning
is the stimulation of artificial demand that even those
who are reasonably sensible buy more than they can
use.   The market requires that luxury and pomp should
be a habit of their lives.[43]

The whole situation may be summed up thus: the
work of the laborer is wasted in two ways: first, he must
make inferior wares which his inferior position forces
him to buy; and second, he must make wares for the
waste of the rich.   People cannot use in any real sense
what they do not need.   This needless, double waste
is forced upon society by the necessities of the market.
The worker thinks of his livelihood because he must,
and the captain of industry thinks of his market because
he must.   To endeavor to do otherwise under the present system would mean starvation to the worker, and
failure to the entrepreneur.[44]   The inevitable result
of the capitalistic system, Morris concluded, is habit-
ually dishonest and therefore degrading work.   Hardly

the remaining 10% is set down as containing poisonous and otherwise noxious in-
gredients.   According to this estimate we are annually consuming a total value of
$10,000,000 in dangerous and deleterious food."
[43]Morris, *Art and its Producers*, p. 13.
[44]*Ibid.*, pp. 14, 35-36.

a carpenter, mason, or weaver can be obtained to do the smallest piece of work well.[45]   Reflection upon the amount of slipshod, careless work apparent to every observer compels sympathy with Morris's impatience. Workmen in reality have become machines.   Everything has become mechanized.   Art cannot be the result of work so done.

Society is not only dishonest in its work and in its attitude toward the worker; it is also dishonest in its distribution of justice.   It pretends, Morris charged, to have equal laws for a free people; yet it often condemns innocent men and women to cruel punishment simply because they have no rich friends to stand by them in their appeal for justice.   This is due to the fact that the Judiciary, which is made up from the higher classes, looks down upon the lower classes.[46]   Neither is justice free.   He who has the most money can purchase the most immunity from the working of the law.   Morris went so far as to say that the magistrates daily abuse their office in the interest of the upper classes by means of a body-guard of professional witnesses and with the help of policemen, who consider it their sacred duty to get hold of prisoners, especially of the lower orders, and convict them at whatever expense to truth and justice.[47] The middle-class conception of law is that it is an impartial power which enforces respect for the due rights of citizens; but from Morris's Socialist point of view, and from the operation of the law in reference to the restriction of free speech, Morris naturally concluded that its real business is to defend property at the expense of personal rights.[48]

[45]Morris, *Hopes and Fears for Art*, pp. 61-62.
[46]*Commonweal*, July 23, 1887.
[47]*Gommonweal*, August 27, 1887.   One is reminded in this connection of the third degree as a means of adding to the reputation of police officers as skilful detectors of supposed crime, and of the absurd principle of judging police officers by the amount of crime or alleged crime that they are able to detect, rather than by the amount of crime that they prevent.   The experience of the Socialists with the law accounts for Morris's conception of the administration of justice.

[48]*Commonweal*, August 27, 1887.   For a good exposition of the American Constitutional basis for overemphasis of property as opposed to personal rights, see J. Allen Smith, *The Spirit of American Government*.

In a very interesting and instructive article entitled "Confusion of Property with Privilege," (*Independent*, August 19, 1909, and reprinted along with a second

Morris's many denunciations of the present epoch and its industrial organization were so severe and often so passionately expressed that one might almost suppose that he was entirely blind to the good accomplished for the civilization of the world in the present era.   But such is not the case.   He was quick to admit that many pre-judices had been broken down, that many lessons had been taught the world which it had before seemed to be incapable of learning.   He realized that some who had been slaves in former times were now free;[49] and that science and invention had subdued the forces of nature and vastly increased the riches of the world.   He saw that increase of knowledge and freedom of thought had accompanied the mastery over nature.[50]   In fact, the material gains of civilization he nowhere undervalued; his vehement insistence was that all of this external prosperity and seeming freedom had been bought at too high a price because they had destroyed the pleasure and happiness of a large class of people upon whose joy-less labor the riches of the age are mainly founded.   His greatest accusation was, let it be repeated, that the modern system had destroyed art, the natural solace of labor, a solace which the workers once had and always should have.   Nature never intended, Morris asserted over and over again, that work should be a repulsive, unrewarded burden.   It should always be a pleasur-able exercise of human energies.   Neither did Nature ever intend that people should become ugly and maimed, ignorant and uncultured in the struggle for existence.

If one remembers Morris's theory of the relation of art to life, and remembers also that Morris never had an ordinary, narrow conception of art, it will be seen that his conclusions regarding the existing order are logical and inevitable.   Art, Morris always insisted, does not

article appearing in the *Independent* for August 26, 1909, by "The Committee to Inquire into the Status of Democracy"), the author, Jesse F. Orton, A.M., LL.B., says: "Privilege is the antithesis of property, a special favor, an exception to the rule of competition and the law of private property."   The Socialist would reply, however, that privilege rests upon the power of capitalistic private property.

[49]Morris, *Hopes and Fears for Art*, p. 86.
[50]Morris, *Architecture*, etc., p. 118.

mean only "painting, and sculpture, and architecture, but the shapes and colors of all household goods, nay, even the arrangements of the fields for tillage and pasture, the management of towns and of highways of all kinds; in a word, . . . all the externals of our life."[51] Look again for a moment at Morris's definition of art as applied to those things which man touches with his labor. Art is the expression of man's joy in his labor. If a man is happy in his work, if he is free to express his soul and its aspirations in the making of things, he will inevitably produce art, just as nature does. And what he produces will be in accord with nature and will add to the fairness of the earth, instead of effacing it or degrading it with ugliness. Consider the uselessness, the hideousness of many things which are made to-day; consider the degradation and the squalor in which many of the workers live, in their laboring hours often crowded into insanitary, filthy factories, in their scant leisure huddled into wretched, miserable slums, or amusing themselves in bestial ways,[52] ill-fed, ill-clothed; and remember that in past days, though under adverse conditions, man produced beauty which shows unmistakable evidences of happiness in the work, and Morris's severe indictment of the industrial order which civilization has organized to do its work, is, in its main outlines, justified. The people have been robbed of their happiness, of their share of life. If things remain as they are, even the higher art, that product of geniuses endowed with the incommunicable gift, will die. The cause of art is the cause of the people. The cause of art is the cause of happiness for mankind. Material civiliza-

---

[51]Morris, *Architecture*, etc., p. 165.

[52]It can hardly be denied that many, if not most working-men and women have neither education enough nor leisure enough—except the leisure of poverty-stricken unemployment,—nor wages enough to secure for themselves much wholesome relaxation or recreation. There is truth incontestible in the exclamation of the Pittsburg steel-worker who said to the investigators of the "Pittsburg Survey": "get a decent working day with decent conditions, then ask him [the working man] to stop drinking." Under similar circumstances a young Englishman said to Sir Edwin Chadwick, the English Poor Law investigator: "Do you, sir, come and live here and you will drink whiskey too." Address on Economics and Trade by Edwin Chadwick, Trans. Nat. Association for the Promotion of Social Science; quoted in B. L. Hutchins, *The Public Health Agitation*, 1833-48, p. 17.

tion certainly appears to have forgotten reverence for the life of man upon earth; and therefore it was Morris's belief that the organization of society must be changed in order to bring to the children of men the beauty, the happiness through art which it is the right of all to enjoy.[53]

[53]Morris, *Hopes and Fears for Art*, pp. 215-16.

CHAPTER III

MORRIS'S CONCEPTION OF A TRUE SOCIETY

To work for a change in the construction of society Morris considered the one duty which he could not leave unperformed. His ideals of a sound social order and his diagnosis of modern civilization brought him logically and inevitably to the conclusion that society could not remain as it was. "I ask you to think with me," said this modern champion of a cause,—the noblest that man may fight for, no less than the cause of happiness and the elevation of mankind,—

I ask you to think with me that the worst which can happen to us is to endure tamely the evils that we see; that no trouble or turmoil is so bad as that; that the necessary destruction which reconstruction bears with it must be taken calmly; that everywhere—in State, in Church, in the household—we must be resolute to endure no tyranny, accept no lie, quail before no fear, although they may come before us disguised as piety, duty, or affection, as useful opportunity and good nature, and prudence or kindness. The world's roughness, falseness, and injustice will bring about their natural consequences and we and our lives are part of those consequences; but since we inherit also the consequences of old resistance to those curses, let us look to it to have our fair share of that inheritance also, which if nothing else come of it will at least bring us courage and hope; that is eager life while we live; which is above all things the Aim of Art.[1]

But before Morris could act with satisfaction to himself, he, like many others, had to tread the evolutionary path. It has been seen that not at once did he find a substitute for the unregulated capitalistic system with its anarchical competition and its general disregard of the claims of brotherhood. In the early days of his groping for a solution of the social problem it will be remembered that he had thought some slow and patient reform might be worked out by those really interested in art and in the life of men. Great social and economic difficulties stood, he well knew, in the way of betterment; but perhaps, he had thought hopefully, he was exagger-

[1]Morris, *Signs of Change*, p. 140.

ating their importance.   Time and the current of things
seemed to be working with him in his early, vague solutions.   In the latter part of the nineteenth century an
undefined discontent over the hideousness engendered
by modern life was evident.   Moreover, a revived interest in art was visible.   The remedy for the blunders
of civilization appeared to be more civilization.   Morris's
simple plan involved but little.   He would have people
first of all sacrifice some of the worthless things they
were so ceaselessly busy about; and for the sacrifice
he would have them embrace and practice simplicity.
Then, without doubt, art would once more flourish, and
with it, happiness for all.[2]   This early conviction explains his statements in his first lectures that something
might be done to raise the arts by teaching men to regard
nature properly, to read history rightly; by teaching
all handicraftsmen to draw carefully, and by interesting
them in the determination to do intelligent and excellent
work.[3]   By these means he had hoped that the public
could be educated to see the difference between "cheap,
nasty" goods and real works of art.   Such discrimination
alone would accomplish much toward killing the large
demand for useless articles,—a demand born of habits
of luxury and the desire for pomp.   Morris's cure for modern evils at first was simplicity of taste and simplicity of
life, a "love for sweet and lofty things."[4]   Simplicity and
right education,—these two were to be the Open Sesame
to give art to all.   To the possible objection that everyone could not buy real works of art nor live in decent
houses built on true architectural principles, his reply in
this period was:

Do away with luxury; live the simple life; begin in your own
homes; keep ever in mind the cause, that is, the democracy of art,
the ennobling of daily and common work, which will one day put
hope and pleasure in the place of fear and pain, as the forces which
move men to labor and keep the world a-going. . . . So to us who
have a Cause at heart, our highest ambition and our simplest duty
are one and the same thing: for the most part we shall be too busy

[2]Morris, *Hopes and Fears for Art*, p. 88.
[3]*Ibid.*, p. 26.
[4]*Ibid.*, pp. 30-32.

doing the work that lies ready to our hands, to let impatience for visibly great progress vex us much; but surely since we are the servants of a Cause, hope must be ever with us, and sometimes perhaps it will quicken our vision so that it will outrun the slow lapse of time, and show us the victorious day when millions of those who now sit in darkness will be enlightened by an *Art made by the people, and for the people, a joy to the maker and user.*[5]

But as Morris went about lecturing on art, and as he worked actively in politics, hope of the realization of his ideals by slow reform of the present industrial order fell away from him. With the death of this hope his words against the present constitution of society became more bold and destructive. The talismanic words, "the rights of property, the necessities of morality, the interests of religion", he realized to be a mere shield, "sacramental words of cowardice" which silenced the consciences of those who uttered them and closed the mouths of social reformers to whom they were spoken.

What is the use [Morris asked passionately] of our civilization, if it is to cultivate us into cowards? Let us answer those feeble counsels of despair and say: we also have a property which your tyranny of squalor cheats us of; we also have a morality which its baseness crushes; we also have a religion which its injustice makes a mock of.[6]

The story of Morris's progress toward Socialism has already been told; it is perhaps enough to repeat here that when Morris saw that nothing could be effectively done in the face of the modern organization of industry to give all men some part in the beauty of life, some share in the happiness which nature intends them to enjoy, he openly advocated the overthrow of the present industrial system, and joined the only body which he could find that advocated the same remedy and had worked out a program for a new social order. The class-consciousness and class-antagonism of the working-men of his day gave rise to the belief that Socialism could be inaugurated in his own time. The sign of that class-consciousness and discontent he saw in the deter-

[5]*Ibid.,* pp. 106, 112-13.
[6]Morris, *Hopes and Fears for Art,* pp. 196-97.

mined agitation of the Trades-Unions and in the many labor troubles of the day.[7]   The evidences of stuggle he took to be the stirring of mature revolutionary forces. He had concluded that the system must in some way be destroyed, else civilization would be destroyed instead. Thereafter he deemed it his supreme duty to assist in spreading discontent.[8]   With palliatives he would have nothing to do at first; he considered them unorganized revolts against a far-reaching organization which would ever brace itself anew with more markets, more machines, more emigration, more sermons on "thrift to lack-alls, of temperance to the wretched."[9]   With the middle-class reform ideal he had equally little patience. The bourgeoisie had been working toward its reform ideal since the Reform Bill of 1832, but in Morris's opinion, they were no nearer to it than a "hayrick to the moon."[10]   Stated in Morris's own words, this middle-class reform ideal was as follows:

There is to be a large class of industrious people not too much refined (or they could not do the rough work wanted of them), who are to live in comfort and receive a kind of education (if they can), and not be over-worked; that is, not over-worked for a working-man; his light day's work would be rather heavy for the refined classes.   This class is to be the basis of society, and its existence will leave the consciences of the refined class quite free and at rest. From this refined class will come the directors or captains of labor (in other words, the usurers); the directors of the people's consciences, religious and literary (clergy, philosophers, newspaper-writers), and lastly, if that be thought of at all, the directors of art; these two classes, with or without a third, the functions of which are indefinite, will live together with the greatest good-will, the upper helping the lower without sense of condescension on one side or humiliation on the other; the lower are to be perfectly content with their position, and there is to be no grain of antagonism between the classes: although (even Utopianism of this kind being unable to shake off the idea of the necessity of competition between individuals) the lower class, blessed and respected as it is to be, will have moreover the additional blessing of hope held out to it, the hope of each man rising into the upper class, and leaving the chrysalis of labor behind him; nor, if that matters, is the lower class to

[7]Morris, *Hopes and Fears for Art*, p. 198.
[8]Morris, *Architecture*, etc., p. 100.
[9]*Ibid.*, pp. 125-26.
[10]*Ibid.*, p. 187.

lack due political or parliamentary power; all men (or nearly all) being equal before the ballot-box, except so far as they may be bought like other things.   That seems to be the middle-class ideal of reformed society; all the world turned bourgeois, big and little, peace under the rule of competitive commerce, ease of mind and a good conscience to all and several, under the rule of the devil take the hindmost. . . . I ask you, is such a hope as that worthy of our boasted civilization with its perfected creeds, its high morality, its sounding political maxims?   Will you think it monstrous that some people have conceived another hope, and see before them the ideal of a society in which there should be no classes permanently degraded for the benefit of the commonweal?   For one thing I would have you remember, that this lowest class of utter poverty lies like a gulf before the whole of the working-classes, who in spite of all averages live a precarious life; the failure in the game of life which entails on a rich man an unambitious retirement, and on a well-to-do man a life of dependence and laborious shifts, drags a workingman down into that hell of irredeemable degradation.   I hope there are but few . . . who can comfort their consciences by saying that the working-classes bring this degradation on themselves by their own unthrift and recklessness.   Some do, no doubt, . . . but we know very well how sorely the mass of the poor strive, practising such thrift as is in itself a degradation to man, in whose very nature it is to love mirth and pleasure, and how in spite of all they fall into the gulf.   What! are we going to deny that, when we see all around us in our own class, cases of men failing in life by no fault of their own . . . as might indeed be looked for in the state of war which we call the system of unlimited competition, where the best campaigning luggage a man can carry is a hard heart and no scruples?   For indeed the fulfilment of that liberal ideal of the reform of our present system into a state of moderate class supremacy is impossible, because that system is after all nothing but a continuous implacable war; the war once ended, commerce, as we now understand the word, comes to an end.[11]

Thus Morris came to a conception of a true society. In his exposition of a sound social order he began with the statement that a society founded on artificial force is wrong, and that no one ought to submit voluntarily to wrong.   So far the earth had never seen a really well-ordered society, for in the past and in the present the very pillar of society was and is artificial force.[12] A society of friend and friend, of well-wishers, of people governed by reason, and conscious always of the needs

[11]Morris, *Architecture*, etc., pp. 185-90.
[12]Morris, *True and False Society*, p. 14.

and aspirations of humanity, the individuals of which recognize fully and discharge faithfully their duties to one another, a society built upon and governed by a coöperative fraternalism, would not need to be held together by force; its own inherent right and reason perform that office. This is the kind of society Morris purposed to have. Apparently he saw no difficulties in the way. That society should be so loftily bound, many believe. To make the ideal work is the problem.

It might be objected also that coöperative fraternalism would submerge the individual for the sake of society. But Morris would not have him yield too much to the state. He must have certain qualities and attributes which need the right conditions for their development. Morris claimed for each individual of a sound social order held together by its own inherent right and reason, first, good health, which he said people at the present time scarcely know the meaning of.

> To feel mere life a pleasure; to enjoy the moving of one's limbs and the exercising of one's bodily powers; to play, as it were, with sun and wind and rain; to rejoice in satisfying the due bodily appetites of a human animal without fear of degradation or sense of wrong-doing; yes, and therewithal to be well-formed, straight-limbed, strongly-built, expressive of countenance—to be, in a word, beautiful. If we cannot have this claim satisfied, we are poor creatures after all.[13]

The claim for good health carries with it the claim to be born healthy, to be born well, without the seeds of disease implanted by the luxury or the poverty or the overwork of an ancestor.[14]   In addition to good health for the individual in a sound society, Morris claimed due education. He did not advocate the sort of education which is in vogue at the present time. This he called class-education, which, in his opinion, failed to make a fully developed man. He wished all people to have a truly liberal education, a continuous and well-balanced development of all of the faculties, whether in the school, in the workshop, or in the field;[15] opportunity, according

[13]Morris, *Signs of Change*, p. 22.
[14]*Ibid.*, p. 23.
[15]*Commonweal*, June 30, 1890.

to capacity, for every child to have his share of the
world's knowledge, historical and scientific, and further,
to be trained in some handicraft or fine art; for Morris
held that the community has the right to benefit by the
special talents which its members possess.[16]   Stated
another way, Morris argued that each person should
have such a liberal education as he could take profitably
and suitably.   Education should include the whole man
in all of his activities.

I want all persons to have manners and breeding according to
their innate goodness and kindness, and not according to the amount
of money which their parents happen to have. . . . I want to be
able to talk to any of my countrymen in his own tongue freely, and
feel sure that he will be able to understand my thoughts according
to his innate capacity; and I want to be able to sit at the table with
a person of any occupation without a feeling of awkwardness and
constraint being present between us.[17]

Since nature demands that the mood of idleness should
be satisfied as well as the mood of energy, Morris believed that the individual in a true society should have
abundant leisure.   All persons who must work some
portion of the day have a right, as Morris put it, to
demand and obtain a rest from their work.   It must be
a leisure long enough to rest body and mind, to give
men time to think, to dream, to imagine.   Due rest
must be accorded even when the workers have honorable and fitting work to do.[18]   Morris did not expect,
however, that all of the leisure granted under his ideal
conditions would be used in resting or in dreaming; it
would often be used in the practise of one of the industrial arts for which men have special capacities, and
at which they could not work if they lacked leisure.
Leisure might also be used for travel, for the expansion
of mind which comes from observing how other people
live.[19]

The fourth claim which Morris made for the individual
of a true social order is embodied in the famous sentence

[16]Morris, *Signs of Change*, pp. 24-25.
[17]Morris, *Architecture*, etc., p. 101.
[18]*Ibid.*, p. 127.
[19]Morris, *Signs of Change*, pp. 24-26.

which many people applaud, but of which they do not always see the signification: "It is right and necessary that all men should have work to do which shall be worth the doing, and be of itself pleasant to do; and which should be done under such conditions as would make it neither over-wearisome, nor over-anxious"[20] Morris held, and rightly, that if this claim could be allowed in its entirety, the face of the world would be changed; discontent and strife and dishonesty would no more be known among men. For the ideal that the work must be worth doing would get rid of the baseness and uselessness which habits of luxury and pomp have brought into the world. Worthwhileness and simplicity are here synonymous. Simplicity would get rid of the tons of rubbish which a false taste and a false standard of life have appeared to make necessary. It would assist to a tremendous degree the art of living worthily.[21] It would teach people not to follow slavishly after fashion; to think for themselves what it is they really desire, and keep them from asking for things made under slavish conditions. In fact, simplicity, if practised by all, would free both the user and the maker.[22]

The second clause of Morris's claim for labor, that the work of the worker should be of itself pleasant to do, embodies his largest ideal. Work unpleasant to do, as has been abundantly shown, Morris held to be degrading to the worker spiritually. From his knowledge of past art and history he was certain that labor had once been a pleasure to common men, and he knew also that nature had so made all animals that they receive pleasure from the exercise of their energies. Since work is so large a portion of the life of man, and indeed some form of it compulsory upon him if he would live, Morris considered that it is just and right that man is so made that he may find his greatest happiness in work. The incentive to work ought never to be to gain leisure from work, as many people hold that it is; for work of itself pleasant to do carries with it its own great reward of

[20]Morris, *Architecture*, etc., p. 108.
[21]Morris, *Hopes and Fears for Art*, p. 28.
[22]Morris, *Architecture*, etc., pp. 110-11.

happiness,[23] "the reward of creation, the wages which
God gets."[24]   The present organization of industry
permits the worker no such reward.   It has indeed won
many triumphs, triumphs which Morris was always
willing to admit,—but he argued that these triumphs
are not great enough to compensate the workers for the
unhappiness resulting from the monotony of their lives,
from their being forbidden all self-expression in their
daily labor.   It should be noted that Morris spoke on
this point without qualification.   It cannot be doubted
that some few workers at least find self-expression in
their work, and that in other cases a different mental
attitude in the worker would make unattractive work
somewhat less unattractive.   It is this claim for men,
the claim for happiness, for a worthy life worthily lived,
which brought Morris to the belief that the cause of
Art is the cause of the people.   The past history of
mankind, the growth of mighty kingdoms and empires,
their fall, their rise in other forms, bade him hope.   "This
tale of the past is a parable of days to come,"[25] and so
believing, he saw visions of a time when heed would be
given to other things besides profit, when care would
be taken that the workers were not degraded by their
work, were not housed in insanitary factories, and in
wretched hovels, ill-fed, ill-clothed, their needs as men
unregarded, their happiness denied. For the realization
of that vision, no sacrifice in his own life was too great.

Morris's claim for labor involves still a third point:
"work done under such conditions as would make it
neither over-wearisome nor over-anxious," or to put
the claim another way: no one who is willing to work
should ever fear a want of such employment as would
earn for him the due necessities of mind and body.[26]
The due necessities for a worker he considered to be:
first, honorable and fitting work; second, decency of
surroundings, which includes good lodging, ample space,
and general order and beauty.   By good lodging Morris

[23]*Ibid.*, pp. 116-17.
[24]Morris, *News From Nowhere*, p. 126.
[25]Morris, *Architecture*, etc., pp. 120, 121.
[26]Morris, *Architecture*, etc., p. 126.

meant that the houses in which the workers live must be well-built, clean, and healthful. By ample space, he meant that there must be garden space even in cities, and that waste places and wilds of nature must be left so far as possible untouched. By order and beauty he meant

that not only must our houses be stoutly and properly built, but also that they must be ornamented duly; that the fields be not only left for cultivation, but also that they be not spoiled by it any more than a garden is spoiled; no one for instance is to be allowed to cut down, for mere profit, trees whose loss would spoil a landscape; neither on any pretext should people be allowed to darken the daylight with smoke, to befoul rivers, or to degrade any spot of earth with squalid litter, and brutal, wasteful disorder.[27]

The third necessity implied in the phrase, "due necessities of mind and body," is leisure, already discussed in another connection.

To Morris all of these claims for labor are fundamental to a civilization worthy of the name. Work of any different sort, done under any conditions short of these, was to him unworthy and degrading to the high spiritual destinies of men.[28]   This ideal, if it could be realized,— and Morris never thought it impossible of fulfillment,— would put an end to the system of "the Devil take the hindmost," by which expression he often described the present industrial order; it would bring in the reign of true society, whose motto is "One for all and all for one."[29]   "Let us be *fellows* working in harmony of association for the common good, that is, for the greatest happiness and completest development of every human being in the community."[30]

Fellowship is the word which best sums up Morris's social teaching. In our epoch there is not fellowship, but mastership. In that beautiful and noble romance, *The Dream of John Ball*, Morris's priest says:

Ah, brothers, what an evil doom is this, . . . to have none to love you and to speak to you, to be without fellowship! Forsooth,

[27]Morris, *Architecture* etc., pp. 126-27.
[28]*Ibid.*, p. 128.
[29]*Ibid.*, p. 129.
[30]Morris, *Signs of Change*, p. 177.

brothers, fellowship is heaven, and lack of fellowship is hell: fellowship is life, and lack of fellowship is death; and the deeds that ye
do upon the earth, it is for fellowship's sake that ye do them, and
the life that is in it, that shall live on and on forever, and each one
of you part of it, while many a man's life upon earth shall wane. . . .

Forsooth, he that waketh in hell and feeleth his heart fail him
shall have memory of the merry days of earth, and how that when
his heart failed him there, he cried on his fellow, were it his wife or
his son or his brother sworn in arms, and how that fellow heard
him and came and they mourned together under the sun, till again
they laughed together, and were sorry between them.   This shall
he think on in hell, and cry on his fellow to help him, and shall find
that therein is no help, because there is no fellowship, but every
man for himself.   Therefore, I tell you that the proud, dispiteous
rich man, though he knoweth it not, is in hell already, because he
hath no fellow and he that hath so hardy a heart that in sorrow
he thinketh not of fellowship, his story is soon but a story of sorrow
—a little change in life that knows not ill. [31]

Morris named three conditions of a reasonable society,
prompted by three questions which he asked of present-
day society.   These questions are: first, does each capable person do his fair share of labor?   Second, is his
share of the wealth produced proportionate to his labor?
Third, is waste of labor avoided in the industrial order
of to-day?   To all of these questions Morris was forced
to answer an emphatic NO.   In his indictment of the
system of competitive commerce he gave considerable
attention to the fact that there is a large class of non-
producers in society; that the producers do not have as
much of the wealth produced as the non-producers; and
that the producers have to work on many useless things
necessitated by the habits of pomp and luxury formed
among the upper classes.   In addition, the workmen
not only have to buy the useless articles they produce
in misery and grinding toil; but they have to pay rent
to their landlords at a higher price proportionally than
the rich are obliged to pay; they give their share to the
middleman; they have to contribute as members of
society their share of the taxes, which amount to a
great deal more than they imagine.   These taxes include payment for wars undertaken in order to force

[31]Morris, *The Dream of John Ball*, p. 30.

markets, and payment for running the government, chiefly for the benefit of the upper classes.   About two-thirds of their pitiful wage is thus forced from them at least partly in the interest of the class which is their master.[32]   In the true social order labor would be duly apportioned; wealth would be duly apportioned; no labor would be wasted.

It is hardly necessary in discussing Morris's conception of a sound society to inquire how far Morris was a Socialist.   It is apparent that he accepted all of the Socialistic creeds and included them in his own broader ideals.   He hated what is called civilization and all of its works, and he wished to see them destroyed.   He had definite ideals for new social relations which should secure the greatest amount of happiness to the individuals living in those relations.   All should be happy in their work, for nature had so made man that a right use of his energies brings him pleasure.   Morris found that the Socialists also hated so-called civilization and wished to destroy it and to set in its place more or less equality of condition and real equality of opportunity. He joined their organization and forthwith and whole-heartedly adopted their program, and studied and used their economic arguments; yet in addition he ever preached his own noble ideals of work-pleasure, of the right of human beings to gain happiness in the work which they are compelled to do in order to live.   This philosophy of pleasure in work most Socialists of his time, with their interest directed to surplus values, scarcely thought of in their eagerness to change the industrial order.   His humanitarian revolt against the misery and the social injustice which is connoted by the word *poverty* and equally by the word *luxury*, he often expressed more eloquently than most Socialists.   But of charity, instead of justice, like them, he would have none.

Do we not know [he asked vehemently] that the greater part of men in civilized societies are dirty, ignorant, brutal, or at best, anxious about next week's subsistence? . . . And we know . . .

[32]Morris, *True and False Society*, pp. 5-11.

that is unfair.   It is an old story of men who have become rich by
dishonest and tyrannical means, spending in terror of the future
their ill-gotten gains liberally and in charity 'tis called; nor are
such people praised; in the old tales 'tis thought the devil gets
them after all.   An old story, but I say, "De te fabula," of *Thee* is
the story told: Thou art the man!   I say that we of the rich and
well-to-do classes are daily doing in like wise; unconsciously, or
half consciously it may be, we gather wealth by trading on the hard
necessity of our fellows, and then we give driblets of it away to
those of them who in one way or another cry out loudest to us.
Our poor laws, our hospitals, our charities, organized and unorganized, are but tubs thrown to the whale, blackmail paid to
lame-foot justice, that she may not hobble after us too fast.[33]

Morris's definition of Socialism is both interesting
and broad.

What I mean by Socialism [he said in one place] is a condition
of society in which there should be neither rich nor poor, neither
master nor master's man, neither idle nor over-worked, neither
brain-sick brain workers nor heart-sick hand workers; in a word,
in which all men would be living in equality of condition, and could
manage their affairs unwastefully, and with complete consciousness that harm to one would mean harm to all—the realization at
last of the meaning of the word *Commonwealth*.[34]

Not indeed a definition couched in the language of political economy, but a definition which embodies all of
his ideals for man and art, which includes all of the aims
and ideals of Socialism.

To Morris, as to other members of his faith, the record
of Socialism may be read in the history of mankind.
Its hope for the future is contained in the same record.
Morris firmly believed in the doctrine of natural historical evolution.   A new world was to be created out
of the materials of the old; and with Marx he declared
that the determining principle of the development of
the new is the proletariat.[35]   The starting-point of
Socialism as a theory of life, based on the evolution of
society, is that man has certain material necessities as
an animal, and that society is the result of man's attempt

[33]Morris, *Architecture*, etc., pp. 128-29.
[34]Morris, *How I Became a Socialist*, p. 7.
[35]William Morris and H. M. Hyndman, *A Summary of the Principles of Socialism*, p. 1.

to satisfy these necessities.   In a word, Socialism has a material basis.

Man as a social animal tends to the acquirement of power over nature, and to the beneficent uses of that power, which again implies a condition of society in which everyone is able to satisfy his needs in return for the due exercise of his capacities for the benefit of the race.   But this economic aim which, to put it another way, is the fair apportionment of labor and the results of labor, must be accompanied by an ethical or religious sense of the responsibility of each man to each and all of his fellows.   Socialism aims, therefore, at realizing equality of condition as its economic goal, and the habitual love of humanity as its rule of ethics.[36]

Association, not competition is therefore the keystone of true society.

Morris, along with other Socialists, always insisted that he could not give any details of how society would be organized under Socialism because he did not know what of the old materials would remain to be cemented in with, and perhaps modify the new.[37]   But a part of the plan of society under Socialism is repeated in many of his lectures.   As he outlines and interprets it, it is as follows:

All would have free access to the means of production of wealth; that is, the lands, plants, and stocks of the community, now owned by the privileged, who exact a high tribute for their use.   Morris accepted the Marxian theory of value and of surplus value without analysis or criticism.[38]   No man has created the land, nor more than a small portion of its fertility; neither can any man build a factory or make the machinery therein except with the assistance of other men, nor can he make use of it alone; he must be able to compel people to use it for his benefit.[39]   Under Socialism, all of these things would be owned in common and would be used by the workers in association, who would then include all honest men; each would receive his share of what was produced. The real problem would be to distribute properly.

[36]Morris, *Four Letters on Socialism*, published in *Poet-Lore*, 7:474.
[37]Morris, *True and False Society*, p. 16.
[38]Karl Marx, *Capital*, pp. 156 ff.
[39]Morris, *True and False Society*, p. 18.

Socialists are divided on this point. One side holds that the State should own all of the means of distribution as well as of production, and allow the use of them to those applying for work. If it charged rent for the privilege of using the raw materials with which to produce wealth, this rent would of course return to the community. Under this system, the State would also organize labor; that is, be its employer. All would have to labor in some form, since there would be no means of satisfying any wants otherwise. Labor would not be wasted, nor prices be above the cost of production. Such an organization, it will readily be seen, would effectually change society. The Socialists of the other side hold that it is not necessary to endeavor to find out exactly what each one contributes to the production of wealth. Instead of a State's overseeing this enormous task, they would have what amounts almost to decentralization. The political unit would be the commune, parish, or guild; a federation of the units would constitute society.[40] The necessary work would be performed by all, and all wealth (and there would be plenty of it) would be held in common. Men's needs are much more alike than are their mental or physical capacities, and are not necessarily determined by the kind or amount of work which each man does.[41] If a person, however, had needs beyond the average, he would have to make some sacrifice to satisfy them; to allow the satisfaction of them otherwise would be to commit a wrong against others in the community.[42]

The question as to how workmen of special faculties were to be rewarded above their fellows, Morris answered in a characteristic manner. He looked at the specially talented workman as desirable to and needed by the community, and since he is so needed, the community would naturally take pains to develop his faculties and satisfy his needs; but not, however, at the expense of other members. The man of special talents, with such

[40]Morris, *True and False Society*, p. 20.
[41]Morris, *True and False Society*, p. 19.
[42]Morris, *Signs of Change*, p. 195.

talents well-trained, would do his work as easily as the average man does his task; and since he had the capacity for it, he would therefore do it better than any other kind of work.   He would also get the most pleasure out of it. Indeed, if he were not permitted to follow his bent, he would probably be unhappy.   And though his work were more special, it does not follow that it would be more necessary.   Morris concluded that the only reward a talented workman could have or would demand was the opportunity to develop his powers and the chance to use them.[43]   The captain of industry, if he were so-called, would have his position because he was fitted for it; indeed, everybody would be in the place he found fitted for.   It would be the duty of society to see that he found that place, for one of the principles upon which the social order was to be founded was that man is happiest in exercising his energies in what he likes best.[44] Just how so accurate a system of vocational guidance was to be worked out and applied neither Morris nor his Socialist friends touched upon.

This view of the new State under Socialism, which Morris distinctly held above the other, is based upon complete equality of condition of every member of society.   Morris named this form Complete Socialism, or Communism.   He did not, of course, hope for the realization of Communism at once; he held it as an ideal and considered it a further development of State Socialism.[45] State Socialism would represent the transition stage between the present organization and Complete Socialism, or Communism, and is necessary as such to teach people how to live in fellowship and practise the religion of humanity.   Under such a regime Morris believed that it would be impossible for one man to be made miserable for the benefit of another, or even for society. He believed also that in such a society it would be easy to live; that is, there would be labor-power to spare, but not unemployment; and that communities could be as

[43]Morris, *Signs of Change*, p. 197.
[44]*Ibid.*, p. 198.
[45]*Ibid.*, p. 201.

rich as they were pleased to be.[46]   Men through all the ages had worked to subdue the forces of nature and to make use of the natural materials of the earth.   The victory of men over nature had been vastly greater in the last two hundred years than ever before; and it is therefore a natural conclusion that people living to-day ought to be far wealthier than in the past.   That there is more wealth is well known; yet it is true at the same time that the majority of people at the present time are poor. Under Socialism, Morris reasoned, everyone would be as wealthy as he wished to be because all would work, because all the labor-power of a community would be utilized; and besides, no one would work wastefully. Everyone would receive the produce of his labor and also his due rest or leisure.   But Morris went further than most Socialists when he said that it is not enough for man to reap the products of his work and to have abundant opportunity to work; he needs in addition some compensation for nature's compulsion that to live he must labor.   With all of these desirable things granted under equality of condition, life would still be unhappy if labor were repulsive.   Work must be a pleasure to make happiness possible for man.   This is Morris's central ideal.   Therefore the first thing after the means of production and distribution are in the hands of the community,—after Socialism, in a word, is established,—that Morris would insist upon would be to make all labor attractive.[47]   This he was quite sure would be a simple thing to accomplish because all would work and nothing would be wasted; society would find a vast amount of labor-power available, which, when utilized, would enable all men to live as they pleased.[48] Fear of starvation need no longer oppress anyone. After the first and most necessary wants were provided for, it would be the duty of society to build up what Morris called the ornamental side of life: its pleasure, physical and mental, scientific and artistic, social and individual, on the basis of work willingly and cheerfully done; but

[46]*Ibid.*, p. 155.
[47]Morris, *Signs of Change*, p. 156.
[48]*Ibid.*, p. 160.

the cardinal point which must never be forgotten is that even the commonest labor must be made attractive.[49]

Now the first condition necessary to make labor attractive, in Morris's opinion, is that it be useful.   In a society in which the religion is humanity, that is, a society in which men feel a responsibility for the life of other men, the fact that the work to be done is useful would aid greatly in sweetening it.   The next thing which would aid in making work pleasurable is that the day's labor in a sound social order can be short.   The most important requisite, however, considering the constitution of man, is variety of work, a point which Fourier also emphasized strongly.   To do the same work day after day, especially if it be mechanical purely, is nothing short of torment.   It is more; it is dehumanizing. Under equality of condition Morris held that nothing would hinder a man from learning and practising as many as three crafts, and varying them as he chooses.[50] The result of giving opportunity for variety in work would cause popular art to flourish again, since it grows out of the necessity which a craftsman feels for varying his work.   In other words, Art is the result of such variety, although Morris always insisted, notwithstanding the undoubted spiritual and cultural power of art, that the pleasure which the workman obtains from an opportunity for self-expression in his labor is more important even than the art which he consciously or unconsciously creates.[51]

Morris would not be true to his ideals if he did not insist upon attractiveness of surroundings in the new social order as well as upon attractiveness of work. Factory work, he recognized, would have to continue to be done; but factories and crowded cities of such hideous-

[49]Morris, *Signs of Change*, p. 161.

[50]It is plain that Morris is here taking an incomplete view of the matter when the coöperative character of most work is considered.   In any case, unless machine industry were abolished, changes from one craft to another would have to be regulated by some authority, as the foreman or superintendent of a shop.   The education which Morris claimed for the true social order would take into account a person's diverse talents, no one of which would be permitted to go to waste from disuse as at present.   Morris, *Signs of Change*, pp. 162-63.

[51]Morris, *Signs of Change*, pp. 164-65.

ness as are found at the present time seemed to him to be quite unnecessary. His plan was to have occupations carried on in industrial colleges, country homes, small towns,—anywhere, in fact, where it would suit the workers. The increased cost of production under his proposed system he did not consider important. In his industrial order it would no longer be a matter of life and death that a certain article be made a penny cheaper one year than the last.[52] The first and only requisite for him was that the work be pleasant. To assist in accomplishing this he suggested that the factories become intellectual centres and that the work of operating machinery be but a small portion of each day's work for any one individual. Dirt, disorder, and cramped quarters need not on any pretext exist. Science rightly applied could annihilate smoke, stench, and noise.[53]

Although Morris had, for the most part, a large, simple way of looking at very complex problems, yet in the matter of rendering labor attractive he endeavored to go into some detail. Some sacrifices would be necessary, he knew, to make labor attractive. For example, all should be willing to do whatever is necessary to raise the standard of life desirable for the community. Society might even have to pass through a period of utilitarianism as the foundation for the fuller and happier life to come.[54]

If the cripple and the starveling disappear from our streets, if the earth nourish us all alike, if the sun shine for all of us alike, if to one and all of us the glorious drama of the earth—day and night, summer and winter—can be presented as a thing to understand and love, we can afford to wait a while till we are purified from the past corruption, and till art arises again amongst people free from the terror of the slave and the shame of the robber.[55]

Of first importance in making labor pleasurable is the right use of machinery. Morris has often been called a reactionary because of what people understand him to have said about the use of machinery in a sound

[52]*Commonweal*, April 6, 1889.
[53]Morris, *Signs of Change*, pp. 166-67.
[54]*Ibid.*, pp. 168-69.
[55]*Ibid.*, p. 169.

society.   Professor Veblen, in his *Theory of the Leisure Class*, criticises both Morris and Ruskin for their doctrine of machinery.   He calls it a propaganda of crudity and wasted effort.   According to Professor Veblen people like hand-made goods because, being honorific, they are held to be superior in point of view, or service-ability, or possibly both, "an exaltation of the defective."[56] Professor Veblen and others who share his opinion evidently understand little of Morris's or Ruskin's ideas of art as the expression by man of his joy in his labor, or of works of art as the expression of man's hopes and aspirations.   It is quite true that Morris objected to machinery, but only as it is used at the present time. He often repeated the words of John Stuart Mill, who said that it is doubtful if all of the mechanical inventions of modern times have done anything to lighten the toil of labor.[57] The key to Morris's attitude to ward machinery is found in his attitude toward man.   He recognized well enough that in the world there is repulsive, unintelligent work which might better be done by machinery than by hand.   As a matter of fact, he did not despise machinery; he welcomed it gladly.   His desire was that all the ingenuity of the inventor should be applied to perfecting machinery to the end that human beings might be relieved of toilsome and disagreeable work. But considering the use of machinery in the present industrial order, Morris came to the conclusion that it had not been invented to save the pain of irksome labor, but to save the *cost* of labor.[58] Morris's point was that machines and railways should be controlled by the rational will,

[56]Thorstein B. Veblen, *The Theory of the Leisure Class*, p. 161.
[57]Morris, *Architecture*, etc., p. 123.
[58]Morris, *Architecture*, etc., p. 183.   "They [the Greeks] did not, for example, comprehend that machinery is the surest means of lengthening the working day. They perhaps excused the slavery of one on the ground that it was the means to the full development of another.   But to preach slavery to the masses, in order that a few crude and half-educated parvenues might become 'eminent spinners', 'extensive sausage-makers', and 'influential shoe-black dealers',—to do this they lacked the bump of Christianity" (Marx, *Capital*, p. 407).   "In so far as machinery dispenses with muscular power, it becomes a means of employing laborers of slight muscular strength, and whose bodily development is incomplete, but whose limbs are all the more supple.   The labor of women and children was, therefore, the first sought for by capitalists who used machinery" (*ibid.*, p. 391).   Marx does not seem to realize that much child and woman labor preceded the machine age.

not the rational will by the machine.   If machines were used to get rid of the most repulsive forms of labor, thus leaving the worker some freedom for intelligent and imaginative work, machines would be an unmixed good. It is *due* use of machinery which Morris preached, not its abolition.   Some things which are now done by machinery he would have done by hand in the new régime; and some of the things which are now done by hand,—those which are oppressive,—he would have done by machinery.[59]   In our epoch we have refrained from using machines for much of the roughest and most pleasureless work because the use of machinery for such work does not pay.[60]   It is the use of machinery to degrade humanity, not to uplift it that Morris decried. Morris had the Greek view of the value of machinery. "If," said Aristotle, "every tool, when summoned, or even of its own accord, could do the work that befits it, just as the creations of Daedalus moved of themselves, or the tripods of Hephaestos went of their own accord to their sacred work, if the weavers' shuttles were to weave of themselves, then there would be need neither of apprentices for the master workers, nor of slaves for the lords."   Likewise, Antiparos, a Greek poet of Cicero's time, hailed the invention of the water wheel as the liberator of female slaves and the restorer of the golden age.[61]

Under a régime of Socialism Morris believed that *due* use would be made of machinery.   In the first efforts of the new and reasonable society to render labor attractive, he assumed that men would go on perfecting machinery to be employed for really useful purposes until they found that they had leisure enough to rejoice in the fact that they were alive, until their mastery over nature was so complete that they no longer feared starvation.[62] Having passed through this stage, they would begin looking about to see how they could make their work more attractive; and then they would discover quite

[59]Morris, *Art and its Producers*, p. 15.
[60]William Morris and E.. Belfort Bax, *Socialism*, etc., p. 306.
[61]Quoted in Marx, *Capital*, p. 406.
[62]Morris, *Signs of Change*, pp. 135-36.

naturally that there was a great deal of pleasure to be derived from doing certain kinds of work by *hand*.[63] The tendency under the competitive system is to extinguish all hand work; but it was Morris's belief that after the elaboration of machinery to its utmost had brought about the simplification of life, the pendulum would swing again in favor of the handicrafts.[64]

It is on the basis of this declaration of faith in the ultimate return of the handicrafts in the future society that the critics pronounce Morris a reactionary who would set us amid a life similar to that lived in mediaeval times. Morris himself declared that if it were reactionary to hate machinery as it is used at the present time, then he was reactionary. But not from the merely aesthetic point of view

which looks upon the ploughman and his bullocks and his plow, the reaper, his wife, and his dinner, as so many elements which compose a pretty tapestry hanging, fit to adorn the study of a contemplative person of cultivation, but which is not worth while differentiating from each other except in so far as they are related to the beauty and interest of the picture. On the contrary, what I wish for is that the reaper and his wife should have themselves a due share of all the fullness of life.[65]

Morris longed for a return to the individual methods of work because, from the manner in which he interpreted history and art, and from his own experience, he was sure that man was happier under such a system of production than under our own with its excessive division of labor and domination over man by machinery. In mediaeval times the workman worked for himself, not for the capitalist; he was the unit of intelligent labor. It has already been pointed out that Morris did not consider nineteenth-century civilization to be an unmixed evil. As a condition of life, production by machinery he did hold to be an evil; but as a means of forcing man to a higher development, he held it to be a benefit. And when men return to production by handicraft, Morris

[63]Morris, *Signs of Change*, pp. 127, 135.
[64]*Ibid.*, p. 33.
[65]Morris, *Architecture*, etc., p. 215.

believed that they would not revert to the simple, rude methods of their ancestors, but that they would use new and improved methods precisely because of what nineteenth-century civilization had taught them, because they would make an intelligent use of its real triumphs, not foolishly discard them.[66]

And though it is undeniable that we [artists] are out of sympathy with the main current of the age, its commercialism, yet we are, (even sometimes unconsciously) in sympathy with that appreciation of history which is a genuine growth of the times, a compensation to some of us for the vulgarity and brutality which beset our lives; and it is through this sense of history that we are united to the tradition of past times.

Past times; are we then reactionists, anchored in the dead past? Indeed, I should hope not; nor can I altogether tell you how much of the past is really dead.   I see about me now evidence of ideas recurring which have long been superseded.   The world runs after some object of desire, strives strenuously for it, gains it, and apparently casts it aside, like a kitten playing with a ball, you say. No, not quite.   The gain is gained, and something else has to be pursued, often something which once seemed to be gained and was let alone for a while.   Yet the world has not gone back, for that old object of desire was only gained in the past as far as the circumstances of the day would allow it to be gained then.   As a consequence, the gain was imperfect; the times are now changed, and allow us to carry on that old game a step forward to perfection: the world has not really gone back on its footsteps, though to some it has seemed to do so.   Did the world go back, for instance, when the remnant of the ancient civilization was overwhelmed by the barbarism which was the foundation of modern Europe?   We can all see that it did not.   Did it go back when the logical and orderly system of the middle ages had to give place to the confusion of incipient commercialism in the sixteenth century?   Again, ugly and disastrous as the change seemed on the surface, I yet think it was not a retrogression into prehistoric anarchy, but a step upward along the spiral, which, and not the straight line, is . . . the true line of progress.

So that if in the future that shall immediately follow on this present we may have to recur to ideas that today seem to belong to the past only, that will not be really a retracing of our steps, but rather a carrying on of progress from a point where we abandoned it a while ago.[67]

Even due use of machinery, however, does not solve the whole problem of making labor attractive.   A ques-

[66]*Ibid.*, 19-20, 219.
[67]Morris, *Art and its Producers*, pp. 42-43.

tion which will naturally be asked is this: How in a society which is based on absolute equality of condition, will the rough and disagreeable work of the world be done? Who will do it? Morris nowhere assumes that there are base, mechanic natures born for the express purpose of doing the rough work for mankind. Nor does he anywhere hint that criminals should be set at the repulsive and dangerous work, for with the overthrow of the present industrial order Morris believed that certainly, if slowly, criminals and prisons would cease to exist. Morris's answer to this question was that the most ingenious machines which the skill of men could invent and perfect would be used in dangerous, rough, and repulsive employments so that as little time as possible might be spent on them. If the work were especially rough, nasty, and exhausting, it seemed to Morris no more than right and reasonable that individuals should take turns at doing it voluntarily. No one ought to be expected to spend all of his time, for example, as a coal-miner or as a fireman. Morris had a fine contempt for men who were afraid of the hardships connected with rough work, provided always that they had leisure and opportunity to vary their work.[68] Some burdensome labor could be lightened by shortening the hours of such labor; some could be left burdensome because it needed to be performed only occasionally; some would lose a measure of its burdensomeness through the worker's consciousness that in performing it he was rendering a service to his fellowmen, especially if appreciation were shown for its doing. As to labor unmitigatedly burdensome, Morris said: "If there be any work which cannot be but a torment to the worker, what then? Well then," Morris answered naively, " . . . let us see if the heavens fall on us if we leave it undone, for it would be better if they should. The produce of such work cannot be worth the price of it."[69] Of course, this is altogether too simple a solution of a perplexing problem, but the critics who find fault with the solutions of social reformers for the evils of the

[68]Morris, *Signs of Change*, pp. 27-28.
[69]*Ibid.*, p. 172.

present system often forget that there are some things which can best be solved when the time comes. Perhaps this is the answer which Morris should have made to this puzzling question. He realized well enough that no details of the new society could be accurately given; yet he was often drawn by curious people into expressing opinions as to what would probably take place in the new industrial order. The thoroughly utilitarian critic could hardly be expected to show great sympathy with Morris's simple answer.

In his details for a sound social order, Morris, as has been shown, was chiefly interested that people should be happy in their work; he placed but little emphasis on the political side of life. He has left a few thoughts on this subject, however, which may be of sufficient interest to be included here.

If people were living in a society of which equality of condition is the watchword, politics, in the usual understanding of the word, would no longer exist.[70] Under the present system, direct coercion is applied to a government of persons. Under Socialism the important thing would be the administration. The conduct of people, except indirectly, would not be the primary concern of the government. Civil law, which is based on private property and deals with things and their domination over persons, would necessarily cease to exist. Criminal law would also tend to die out.[71] Whatever laws there might be would be much simpler than those now known; and nearly all of them would be concerned with personal protection. Private property having disappeared, only the *use* of property by the public would have to be considered.[72] The substitution of association for competition would also operate on nations as it would on individuals. When living for profit ceases, the necessity of holding together large masses of men in order to further the interests of a special locality or nation would no longer be essential. Even the word *nation* would cease to have any meaning except as indicating a race, lan-

[70]Morris, *Four Letters on Socialism*, in *Poet-Lore*, 7:474.
[71]William Morris and E. Belfort Bax, *Socialism*, etc., p. 290.
[72]Morris, *Four Letters on Socialism*, in *Poet-Lore*, 7:543.

guage, or geographical expression. As political entities, nations would disappear. According to Morris, who looked upon State Socialism as a transitional phase between the present order and the future society under Complete Socialism, or Communism, society as a whole would become a federation of a variety of communities. The unit of the federation would be the township, or the local guild, which would manage its affairs in direct assemblies, the majority prevailing. A central body, if there were one, would be chiefly concerned in guarding the principles of a sound and reasonable society. The central body would become entirely unnecessary after the religion of humanity, the ethics of Socialism, had permeated the whole of civilization and men had learned to live as friends and not as enemies. Between the unit and the central body there would be, as occasion arose, federations of certain communities. Public communication between the members of the federation would have to be carried on by delegations. All competent citizens would take part in the business which concerned the public; but no one of these would receive any special honors or any special power over anyone. In the process of evolution in a society managed as this one would be, all government would tend to disappear, leaving each ward, parish, or local guild to manage its own affairs directly and with friendly correspondence with other units as occasion might dictate.[73] The difficulties that frequently arise in America over the relative merits of State rule and Home rule suggest that Morris's plan might not be sufficient until all mortals have become thoroughly reasonable, honest, and unselfish. His answer to this might have been: "My plan would work with a race of real democrats"; which suggests the persistent need that both Socialists and other reformers should emphasize continually the ethics of democracy.

To the question as to what would be done with the drones under the new régime, since heredity and dislike of work might reasonably be expected to continue, Morris answered indirectly that even if there were some

[73]Morris, *Four Letters on Socialism*, in *Poet-Lore*, 7:544.

idle people in consequence of these two influences, they could not possibly equal the number of idlers at the present time, counting the non-producing classes and those unfortunates in the reserve army who indeed cry out for work, but failing to find it, are punished by starvation and the workhouse. Since human happiness consists in the pleasurable exercise of our energies, Morris did not fear that an over-plus of idlers would afflict a sound society. The instinct for workmanship implanted in human beings, and the moral sense which all possess to some degree, which would be promoted and developed by education, would combine to eliminate the idler.

As to the ethics of Socialism as a daily guide, it is only necessary to say that for Morris it was contained in the word *Fellowship*, the duty of man to his neighbor; the religion of Socialism is the duty of man to the race of men.[74] When Morris was questioned by the Reverend Dr. Bainton on the subject of religion in the future society, he answered:

I am an artist, or workman, with a strong inclination to exercise what capacities I may have, and a determination to do nothing shabby if I can help it; or if I do do something shabby, to admit that I have done so, and to be sorry for it. This appears to me to be the Socialist religion, and if it is not morality, I do not know what it is.[75]

Like all Socialists, Morris advocated the economic independence of women, a logical consequence of a society founded upon equality of condition. Every woman would be as free as every man to earn her own living. But Morris held that there could not be any real competition between the sexes because of the very principles upon which society would rest. Women would do the work which they could do best, and they would be trained to do it. They would neither wish to seek, nor would they get work which men could perform better than they.[76] The present marriage system, characterized as

[74]William Morris and E. Belfort Bax, *Socialism*, etc., p. 298.
[75]Morris, *Four Letters on Socialism*, in *Poet-Lore*, 7:546.
[76]*Commonweal*, May 28, 1887.

it is by the economic dependence of women, would disappear, Morris believed, when competitive commerce disappeared; and its place would be taken by marriage, based not on a contract enforcible by law, but by an association which could be terminated at will.   Morris, along with other Socialists, believed that the development of a social conscience would keep married people from oppressing each other.[77]

It can readily be seen from Morris's slight discussion of the woman problem that he was not especially interested in women and their cause. His pronouncements are entirely uncritical. He merely accepted the Socialist teachings on the subject with no subtractions or additions. Socialists include the equality of women in all of their programs; yet it is clear that this is an inevitable result of the position which they assume, and not because they are, as a party, really interested in the cause of women. Some confirmation of this view is to be found in a well-expressed protest by John Spargo in 1908 against the Socialistic lack of earnest and active interest in the Woman movement.[78]

As to how the transition from the present organization of society to Socialism would take place, Morris was not very explicit. While he was a member of the Socialist League and was using all of his energies to usher in the new day in his own lifetime, he would have nothing to do with palliative measures. Even after his hope of immediate revolution was crushed, for a time he advocated complete abstention from Parliamentary action as a means of bringing in the new order. He confined his work, and advised the members of the League to do likewise, to education toward Socialism. When enough Socialists had been made, the way, he thought, to the new social order would be easy to travel.

One man with an idea in his head is in danger of being considered a madman: two men with the same idea in common may be foolish,

[77]William Morris and E. Belfort Bax, *Socialism*, etc., pp. 299-300.
[78]John Spargo, *Woman and the Socialist Movement*, in *International Socialist Review*, 8:449-55. A little later, in May, 1908, the American Socialist Party made the following a part of their demands: "Unrestricted and equal suffrage for men and women, and we pledge ourselves to engage in an active campaign in that direction" (*International Socialist Review*, 8:763).

but can hardly be mad; ten men sharing an idea begin to act; a hundred draw attention as fanatics, a thousand and society begins to tremble; a hundred thousand and there is war abroad, and the cause has victories tangible and real; and why only a hundred thousand? Why not a hundred million and peace upon the earth?[79]

During the last six years of his life, Morris, while he did not cease to believe in educating people in the principles of Socialism, and indeed worked unceasingly in that direction to the very end of his life, came to acquiesce in measures for the relief of the workers. These, of course, had in most cases to be obtained through Parliamentary action. He kept always in mind, however, the ultimate ideal, looking upon relief measures not as having any permanent value, but as stepping stones to the assumption by the community of all the means of production and exchange. He had failed to realize up to this time that even small reforms which raise the standard of physical life, also raise the moral standard and are therefore steps upward and onward toward a new day. He saw, but grudgingly indeed, that Socialists had to look at the transition period from the practical point of view.

Doubtless [he said] there will be much trouble and blundering over the carrying of society into this stage; and that is why, I think, we may expect Democracy, which no longer has any principles, nothing but a vague instinct pushing us on, to do something for us. We want the dying old system to make the experimental blunders for us that the new order may set in right, which it can do because its action is based on principle.[80]

Morris realized fully in the end that political means were the only means available at the present time; that it was necessary to create a party with delegates in the House of Commons, the party to have complete control over the delegates. The party of reaction, as the Socialist party grew in strength and in numbers, would have to make concession after concession until there would be hardly anything more to concede. Morris came to agree with the program of palliation which the

[79]Morris, *Architecture*, etc., p. 197.
[80]Morris, *Four Letters on Socialism*, in *Poet-Lore*, 7:476, 477.

Social Democratic Federation was advocating, for he saw that such a program was necessary.[81]

Morris was broad enough to see that the ideal which he had conceived of a sound and a reasonable society was not the final ideal and goal of society.   A firm believer in evolution, he necessarily held that in the end Socialism must give way to even higher developments in which the ever-growing aspirations of man would have full play.   Yet so far as he was concerned, he could imagine no society beyond that which would endeavor to elevate men to a plane where all could be happy, and where all could find that happiness in their work.[82]

A chapter on Morris's idea of a sound social order would not be complete without some detailed mention of his Utopian romance, *News From Nowhere*.   Although he always insisted that it was impossible to give details as to how the new industrial order would work because no one could tell how much of the present system would be carried over into the future, he nevertheless was persuaded to make an attempt to satisfy the story-desiring instincts of the subscribers of the *Commonweal*, the organ of the Socialist League.   To picture a sound society more or less according to his ideas, he published *News From Nowhere*, his Utopian romance.   He has been severely criticized because in this romance more than elsewhere perhaps he reverted to traditions of labor in operation in the fourteenth century; or, as it seems to some, because he attempted to make the thirteenth or fourteenth century follow logically on the twenty-second, for *News From Nowhere* is laid in a future some two hundred years or more from the present.   It is certainly true that Morris has given something of a mediaeval tone to his story, but chiefly by means of verbal reference to the Middle Ages,—references to costume, and general simplifications of life.   It must be remembered in this connection that Morris was a born lover of the mediaeval period.   The remains of its beautiful art were evidence to him that man had been happy in

---

[81]*Justice*, January 24, 1884.
[82]William Morris and E. Belfort Bax, *Socialism*, etc., pp. 320-21.

those days, and that his work had been a pleasure to him.   Morris did not underrate the fact that there had been cruelty, oppression, and serfdom, and that man had but a very imperfect control of the forces of nature; but the marvellous architecture of the Middle Ages told him, as it has told others, that the workmen of to-day, with all of their free presses, popular suffrage, railways, and their liberty to live how and where they please, are less free in reality than the artist-workers of the fourteenth century, who though imprisoned in a system, were yet at liberty within that system to express their fancy, their imagination, their aspiration.   Slaves they might have been in body; yet they were free in soul, free to work in harmony with nature, free to guard the natural fairness of the earth by the creation of beauty which attempted to equal its own, which expressed their deep reverence for it.   So the spirit of the new days reflected in Morris's Utopia is a passionate love of the fairness of the earth, a keen pleasure in all the life of the world, undying interest in the recurring seasons and the changeful weather and in every detail of life.   Architecture, and all the popular arts,—truly popular there,—express the generous and abounding life of a happy people who are not, it must be admitted, troubled in their joy by any problems of metaphysics or over-intellectuality of any sort.   They have won, not "freedom from labor," but "freedom *in* labor"; and their reward for their labor is life, the joy of creation, "the wages which God gets."[83] They need take no trouble for their lives; for they have profited in a sensible way by all the mastery over nature accomplished by the nineteenth and following centuries. Indeed they are sometimes troubled by the ghost of a fear that work may become scarce, until they remember that they may always express their energy and their souls in added ornament.[84]   Labor, of course, is thoroughly humanized, and the art-instinct which is common to all men is gratified to its fullest extent.   The true reign

[83]Morris, *News from Nowhere*, p. 126.
[84]*Ibid.*, pp. 126-27.

of democracy of art, the social aim of Morris, is realized in *Nowhere*.

We live amid beauty without any fear of becoming effeminate; we have plenty to do, and on the whole enjoy doing it. . . . England was once a country of clearings among the woods and wastes with a few towns interspersed, which were fortresses for the feudal army, markets for the folk, gathering places for the craftsmen. It then became a country of huge and foul workshops and fouler gambling dens, surrounded by ill-kept, poverty-stricken farms, pillaged by the masters of work-shops. It is now a garden, where nothing is wasted, and nothing is spoiled, with the necessary dwellings, sheds and workshops scattered up and down the country, all trim and neat and pretty. For indeed, we should be too much ashamed of ourselves if we allowed the making of goods, even on a large scale, to carry with it the appearance even of desolation and misery.[85]

Large towns as such, and country life as such have almost disappeared. The one has merged into the other. Factories are called banded work-shops; and the people collected there work in them, not because they wish to use power or to save expense, but because they find it altogether convenient.[86]

The workmen in Morris's ideal society, who are of course artists, are all handsome of form and face, healthy, well-mannered, intelligent, educated as they should be. They have sound minds in sound bodies. The dustman can bow as gracefully and as naturally as the traditional Spanish cavalier. The women also are all beautiful, graceful, and unaffected; their manners are most charming, and their interest in life is as keen as the men's. Naturally in a society of equals there is no question of woman's rights. There is no woman movement in Utopia. The only strife between the sexes is the world-old strife which the love of man for woman engenders. No courts of law are needed, however, to enforce contracts of sentiment or passion. It is not exactly a "do as you like world" as Mr. Hobson would have us believe; but a world in which moral obligations are summed up in a law which runs "Love thy neighbor as thyself."[87] There

[85]Morr s, *News from Nowhere*, pp. 100-01.
[86]*Ibid.*, pp. 66-67.
[87]Hobson, *John Ruskin, Social Reformer*, p. 306; and Morris, *Signs of Change*, pp. 81-82.

is no competition between the sexes because all are economically independent; all must work, but women do the work for which they are best fitted and by which they can best serve society.   Morris plainly thought them best fitted for the art of keeping the house and home.   "Don't you know," Morris had the Sage of Bloomsbury say, "that it is a great pleasure to a clever woman to manage the house skilfully, and to do it so that all the house-mates about her look pleased, and are grateful to her."[88]   In Utopia such is everyone's interest in the ordinary details of life that even the men are interested in the process of cooking, and many of them are experts in the art.[89]   Thus it seemed quite natural to Morris that women should take without revolt the role of home-maker and teacher.   Relieved from sordid anxieties as to what was to become of her children in the future,

the ordinary healthy woman (and almost all of our women are both healthy and at least comely), respected as a child-bearer and rearer of children, desired as a woman, loved as a companion, unanxious for the future of her children, has far more instinct for maternity than the poor drudge of past days could ever have had; or than her sister of the upper classes, brought up in affected ignorance of natural facts, reared in an atmosphere of mingled prudery and prurience.[90]

Morris's Utopia, as was inevitable, provided critics with deadly ammunition against socialistic ideas and Morris's exposition of them.   The makers of ideal societies always go astray, it seems, because they endeavor to treat complex matters in an absurdly simple manner. Morris's treatment of the sex problem in *News From Nowhere* is a shining example of the usual error.   The difficulty is that the idealist who writes the Utopia can have no more than a bird's eye view of his state, while the critics have infinitely minute views of the present society. Some points are sure to be slighted in the building of the fancy picture. The principle may be

[88]*Ibid.*, p. 84.
[89]*Ibid.*, p. 85.
[90]Morris, *News From Nowhere*, p. 86.

right in every way, but the method of applying it may
be wholly wrong and confusing.   This is glaringly the
case with Morris's Utopia.   Hence the justness from
one angle of such a criticism, for example, as that which
Mr. Maurice Hewlett makes on *News From Nowhere.*[91]
In the first place, Mr. Hewlett objects because the twenty-
third century is followed by the fourteenth,—because
the Utopia has been made up of "rejuvenated relics."
This, of course, is only a half-truth.   The mediaeval
atmosphere in Morris's story is after all no more than an
atmosphere.   Its introduction is without doubt to be
explained on the ground that building imaginary societies
is always more or less subjective proceeding.   That
Morris was a passionate admirer of the Middle Ages has
been sufficiently emphasized.   He was besides an artist
with an artist's demands and artist's point of view, although these facts should not prejudice any fair minded
person.   Morris's critics are prone to forget that he
would retain all of the blessings which the system of
competition has conferred upon man and add to them
art and beauty.   And these are of no age.

Another criticism made upon Morris by Mr. Hewlett
is that Morris exaggerated the dependence of human
nature upon its environment, and that he assumed that
human welfare is conditioned by the physical.   Consequently Mr. Hewlett accuses Morris,—and he is not
the only accuser,—of creating a materialistic, *earthy*
paradise instead of an earthly one.   The people of *Nowhere*
are artistic and sensuous, not serious and speculative.
There is too much happiness, too much wealth, too much
beauty, too much art, too much disregard of death as a
fact and of life as a riddle.   Morris's people do not look
behind nature, simplicity, and truth; they want none of
the shadows of life.   Indeed, they are exquisitely ob-
livious of the fact that there are shadows, that explana-
tions and justifications are a part of the universe.   The
eternal why of all unhappy people is never spoken.   To
Mr. Hewlett all that is worth gaining must be won by
constant striving and by constant renunciation.   "Pare

[91]Maurice Hewlett, in *National Review*, 17:818.

off what is clay and clogs aspiration; foster what is ether and strains toward its fount." A worthy and noble ideal indeed, and one to which Morris would have subscribed entirely. But Mr. Hewlett and other critics who find too much of material happiness in *News From Nowhere* forget that before men can renounce, they must first be men; they must not be degraded animals fighting in misery and squalor for the wherewithal to satisfy the cravings of hunger, day after day and year after year, life meaning nothing else but work hardly got, and bread eaten amid tears and degradation. Was it not Aristotle who said, "It is needful first to have a maintenance, and then to practise virtue?" Surely history teaches that man cannot be raised morally or intellectually to any perceptible degree until he has first been placed on a sound physical basis of existence. Much as he loved beauty, Morris was pleading for the lives of men, not merely for the creation of a little more beauty in the world except as it stood for increased life. He saw that the true cause of poverty is industrial and that therefore the remedy must also be industrial. Material growth must precede moral growth. Individuals cannot, however much they are willing to renounce, raise the moral tone of society as a whole. The most rigid introspection accompanied by the severest asceticism is of no avail unless the social conditions are such as to raise the moral tone of the whole people. The spiritual life of a people has some dependence upon the material conditions in which that people live.[92] No doubt Morris was led into many absurd little by-paths in his attempt to create a picture of ideal society; but he certainly did not altogether disdain the spiritual life of men when he pleaded for art, or for Socialism in order that we might have art, or when he built up a beautiful *Nowhere* in which all were interested in life; where all were happy in their work. "Love thy neighbor as thyself," the religion of humanity, if truly practised, might, it must ever be remembered, demand as much education and renunciation as the severest faith. The closing words of *News*

[92]Alfred Russell Wallace, *Social Environment and Moral Progress.*

From Nowhere are significant testimony of Morris's un-
wavering belief in the high destiny of man, as well as a
silencing answer to his critics:

> You cannot be of us; you belong so entirely to the unhappiness of
> the past that our happiness would weary you.   But go back again,
> now you have seen us, and your outward eyes have learned that in
> spite of all the infallible maxims of our day, there is yet a time of
> rest in store for the world, when mastery shall have changed into
> fellowship,—but not before.   Go back again, then, and while you
> live you will see all around you people engaged in making others
> live lives which are not their own, while they themselves care noth-
> ing for their own real lives,—men who hate life though fear death.
> Go back, and be the happier for having seen us, for having added
> a little hope to your struggle.   Go on living while you may, striv-
> ing, with whatsoever pain and labor needs must be, to build up
> little by little the new day of fellowship, and rest and happiness.

CHAPTER IV

Morris's ideals, both as a destructive and a constructive thinker, have their origin in the fact that he was by temperament and training an artist. His discontent with social and industrial conditions and his ideals for the society of the future find their source in the demands of his beauty-loving soul. The cause of art led him to the cause of the people. This, and the fact that he was a man of wealth, make his social teaching not less, but more significant.

The contrast between the cheap and nasty work done in the nineteenth century and the beautiful relics of the work done in the Middle Ages set Morris to thinking upon the problem of why the worker of long ago inevitably produce beauty, whereas the worker of the present day inevitably produces ugliness. Not only did Morris find ugliness in articles needed in everyday life, but he also found it in the architecture destined for some measure of permanency. The production of ugly wares and ugly buildings he saw accompanied by a blighting carelessness of the aspects of nature; by a disregard for beautiful landscapes, for blue, unsmoked skies, for clear, unbefouled rivers; by unreverence even for the works of beauty which the handicraftsmen of the Middle Ages had created and left in the form of noble cathedrals, humble grey churches, and here and there a little grey cottage. He concluded from his study of social and industrial conditions that the end of modern life is profit.

Morris's ideas of the relation of art to life led him by a direct road to his social theories. His artist-soul found everything made by the hand of man either beautiful or ugly, depending upon the conditions under which it is made: beautiful if the worker is free to express his soul in his work; ugly if his individuality is fettered; beautiful if he takes pleasure in the making; ugly if his work has been done under material compulsion by mechanical

toil. Nature has implanted in man an instinct for workmanship which, when given free play, brings happiness
and eager life to the worker. Indeed, all excellent work,
in the broad conception of Morris, in the carrying out
of which there has been due regard for *human* cost as
apart from industrial or business cost, is art. Work
done under such conditions will be happy work; and
happy work is art. But the present organization of
society does not allow free play to the inborn instinct
for workmanship; and the consequence is unhappiness
and degradation for the worker. One of the human needs
of man is that he should have beauty to react on his soul.
In the conception of Morris, this need carries with it
the right to beauty, the right to demand of life and of
society that the individual be able to enjoy the work
which nature compels him to do in order to live. Capitalism is unfavorable, however, to allowing a workman
pleasure in his work. It does not ask or permit him to
express his imagination in his daily task; it asks him
only to run its machines and to buy its ugly, mechanical,
soulless products. It exploits him, moreover, to a degree
which forbids him to have beauty in any form in his life.
He may not have the joy of creating beauty, the joy of
possessing beauty, nor the joy of understanding beauty.
Yet the worker, misused as he is, does not suffer alone;
all society suffers with him. Even the rich, though they
desire it ardently, cannot have popular art; for popular
art is a social product depending upon art traditions
and art instincts, both of which have been killed by the
capitalistic system of production. Only the higher forms
of art now exist,—forms utterly meaningless to the poor
and but half understood by the rich, because the higher
forms depend upon the lower, upon popular art. Society
is richer under the modern system, but it has less wealth,—
less well-being,—less happiness. Over and over Morris
insisted that man has a right to the fullest, freest life;
he has the right to enjoy, the right to be happy; and he
is so constructed that he can find enjoyment and happiness in their completest sense, only in his daily work.
Competitive Commerce, founded on force, anchored in

coercion and dishonesty, denies man his birthright. Once the unit of intelligent work was a whole man; now, perchance, it takes a hundred men to make one article; and every man must do his hundredth part and only that through all his days.   No human interest can lend its glow to such work.   The life and character of each individual worker can but be narrowed and degraded under a system so organized.   Both life and work have been inevitably mechanized and dehumanized.   Machine work makes machine men.   The product of pleasureless toil bears the marks of the degradation and of the unhappiness of the worker in its sham, meaningless ornament, in its cheap and shoddy make-up.   But this is not all.   Commerce carried on by competition is fruitful of waste; waste in the number of the unemployed crying for work; waste in people not doing the thing for which they are fitted; waste in the production of useless wares demanded by false taste and false, unsimple standards of life; waste of life in the long hours spent in insanitary workshops.   The questionable foundation and methods of Competitive Commerce are, moreover, reflected in the spiritual life of the whole people.   Here, then, lies the basis of Morris's hatred of what he named civilization.   Civilization has forbidden man to be happy because it has reduced him and the orbit of his life to a mechanism; it is founded upon dishonesty and coercion, giving a few measureless power over the many; it makes its people enemies each to each; it has, as a final result, debased the work and the spiritual life of the people.

Morris's own experiences as an artist made him see as in a crystal held in his hand what it is that man needs for his happiness, and to insist passionately on man's right to enjoy, to live an eager life.   For without being a psychologist he realized a great truth that psychology teaches, namely, that

wherever the process of life communicates an eagerness to him who lives it, there the life becomes genuinely significant.   Sometimes it is more knit up with motor activities, sometimes with the perceptions, sometimes with the imagination, sometimes with reflective thought.   But wherever it is found, there is the zest, the tingle, the excitement of reality; and there is importance in the only real and possible sense in which importance anywhere can be.[1]

Morris's own daily experience, as he went on his beauty-worshipping way, taught him what it is that makes life significant, eager, and complete.   Many men realize in themselves and for themselves what it is that makes life worth-while for them; but not on all does a great light shine and show them and cause them to feel in a vital and dynamic way what makes life real for others.   When the light does so shine, the result is a great prophet and a great democrat.   In words which Morris might have spoken, Professor Josiah Royce has described the feelings of the average man toward the life and needs of others, at the same time making an eloquent appeal for sympathy with our fellow-creatures:

What, then, is our neighbor?   Thou hast regarded his thought, his feeling, as somehow different from thine.   Thou hast said, "A pain in him is not like a pain in me, but something easier to bear." He seems to thee a little less living than thou; his life is dim, it is cold; it is a pale fire beside thy burning desires. . . . So, dimly and by instinct hast thou lived with thy neighbor, and hast known him not, being blind.   Thou hast made [of him] a thing, no Self at all. Have done with illusion, and simply try to learn the truth.   Pain is pain, joy is joy, everywhere as in thee.   In all the songs of the forest birds, in all the cries of the wounded and dying, struggling in the captor's power; in the boundless sea where the myriad of water-creatures strive and die; amid all the countless hordes of savage men; in all sickness and sorrow; in all exultation and hope, everywhere, from the lowest to the noblest, the same conscious, burning, wilful, life is found, endlessly manifold as the fires of the sun, real as these impulses that even now throb in thine own little selfish heart.   Lift up thine eye, behold that life, and then turn away, and forget it as thou canst; but, if thou hast *known* that, thou hast begun to know thy duty.[2]

It is Morris's distinction and eternal honor that not only did he come to know his duty, but he accepted it with unflinching courage and sublime self-effacement. The present industrial order, be believed, forbids men to be happy; all men, he reasoned, have a right to be happy and to enjoy life; if this be true, then the prevail-

[1]William James, *Talks on Psychology and Life's Ideals*, p. 234.
[2]Josiah Royce, *The Religious Aspect of Philosophy*, pp. 152-62.

ing system must be changed in some way. Socialists, he found, were working on the material side of these very problems; they had a constructive program to substitute for the system they would destroy. Not as a dreamer, not as an impractical poet and mere enthusiast did Morris join the Socialist movement. Too much of faith he, with his Utopian brother Socialists, had indeed in the ripeness of the regenerative forces, in speedy change; yet who can wholly censure him for doing his duty as he saw it? Not without result did the Socialists in that decade labor, when with Utopian ardor and Utopian plans they hoped the wrongs of centuries might be redressed in a day. Many a dull Respectable living in fatted complacency upon the misery of thousands, his mind closed by class bias, had his sensibilities quickened and his sympathies aroused to the needs of the poor and to the waste of the system of Competitive Commerce; to the need of legislation for the regulation of capitalistic industry and commerce. Out of the passionate eloquence of the persistent Socialist agitator has been born a new interest in labor problems, a new impulse toward the humanization of the life of the degraded poor.

It is not necessary here to recapitulate the constructive program of the Socialists, which Morris accepted entire when he joined their ranks. His own claims for a true social order, inspired by a passion for the wholeness of life, are broader than theirs, including all of their aims and ideals, and more. The demands which he made for men,—healthy bodies, due education, fit work for mind and body, duly adjusted to individual capacity, and a beautiful world to live in,—carried to their logical conclusion would mean a social organization which takes into account not first and always the business cost, regardless of the human cost; not man as a means alone of production, but first and always the *human* cost, the *social* cost; for the wealth of a society can only be meaured in the well-being of its members, physically, intellectually, and spiritually. Profit and riches should find no place in such a calculation. Morris saw very clearly that a people with an abundance of real wealth, moreover, would always have a proper appreciation of the relation of the physical to the spiritual.   The world cannot be regenerated spiritually except on the basis of sound conditions of work and life.   A society founded on dishonesty and force denies a sound physical life to the majority of its members, and contaminates all spiritually from the very dishonesty inherent in its being; neither can people be truly virtuous nor aspire to spirit-heights when they are cold and hungry.

Morris's greatest ideal was that men should be happy in their work.   The relation of art to life has its greatest significance when stated in such terms, for Art is nourished not by theory, but by life.   Happiness for men has been the subject of many a foggy metaphysical treatise which has left the reader more bewildered and more unhappy over life's riddles than before.   Morris has a noble ideal of work-happiness which all can understand.   This simple ideal for the right of every man to be happy in the labor which Nature compels him to do and which Nature intended he should find pleasure in, no one has ever pleaded more earnestly for, nor battled more strenuously to attain than did Morris.   This is his vital and dynamic thought which his admirers cannot but turn prophet over, saying that it must take its place, as the years go by, with the utterances of the world's greatest thinkers, and that it will grow more and more significant in the lives of men until, though the way may be long, society may be so organized that it will permit to each one of its members that happiness which Morris's ideal seeks.

Morris has often been called a dreamer, and his social thought has by some been considered of little power and influence because he was a poet and an artist and not a specialist in economics.   How could a poet and an artist, ask those who separate the literary men from the practical, and consider that a person who loves beauty and makes poetry is necessarily unable to think,—how could a poet and artist, a man who openly professed to admire the Middle Ages beyond the highly-polished and intellectual nineteenth century, be expected to say anything of worth on a subject of which he did not even know the

language, the technical terms?   The simple mind of the
poet and artist had surely better stay among his old-
world poems and his soft-toned tapestries and his glow-
ing stained-glass.   Many there have been of the world's
Unseeing who have voiced such regrets, but certainly
gratuitously.   Though not a specialist in physiology,
Morris has uttered a truth which that science has formulated; though not a specialist in psychology, he has
uttered a truth which that science has formulated; and
though not a student of economics until after his own
social thought had been matured, his broadest views and
noblest aims nevertheless coincide with those of many
of the ablest of our economic students of the social problem.   Morris was not less a thinker because he used his
sympathetic imagination as well as his reason, because
he left averages and statistics to intellects which deify
them, but are too often unable to realize their import.
Statistics must be reduced to terms of humanity and to
rules of conduct before they can be made to yield the
whole truth.   This was Morris's belief.   Read what he
says of averages:

I don't want to make too much of the matter of money-wages
apart from the ghastly contrast between the rich and poor which is
the essence of our system; yet remember that poverty driven below
a certain limit means degradation and slavery pure and simple.
Now I have seen a statement made by one of the hopeful men of the
rich middle class that the average yearly income of an English
working man's household is one hundred pounds.   I don't believe
the figures because I am sure that they are swollen by wages paid
in times of inflation, and ignore the precarious position of most
working men; but quite apart from that, do not, I beg of you, take
refuge behind averages; for at least they are swelled by the high
wages paid to special classes of workmen at special places, and in
the manufacturing districts by the mothers of families working in
factories,—to my mind a most abominable custom,—and by other
matters of like kind, which the average-makers leave you to find
out for yourselves.   But even that is not the point of the matter.
For my part the enormous average of one hundred pounds a year
to so many millions of toiling people, while many thousands who do
not toil think themselves poor with ten times the income, does not
comfort me for the fact of a thousand strong men waiting at the
dock-gates down at Poplar the greater part of the working day, on
the chance of some of them being taken on at wretched wages, or

for the ordinary wage of the farm laborer over the greater part of England being ten shillings per week, and being considered ruinous by the farmers also; if averages will content us while such things as this go on, why stop at the working classes?   Why not take in everybody, from the Duke of Westminster downwards, and then raise a hymn of rejoicing over the income of the English people? I say let us be done with averages and look at lives and their sufferings, and try to realize them: . . . [not] to console ourselves with averages for the fact that the riches of the rich and the comfort of the well-to-do are founded on that terrible mass of undignified, unrewarded useless misery, concerning which we have of late been hearing a little, a very little; after all we do know that is a fact, and we can console ourselves by hoping that we may, if we are watchful and diligent . . . greatly diminish the amount of it.   I ask you, is such a hope as that worthy of our boasted civilization with its perfected creeds, its morality, its sounding political maxims?   Will you think it monstrous that some people have conceived another hope, and see before them the ideal of a society in which there should be no classes permanently degraded for the benefit of the commonweal?   For one thing I would have you remember, that this lowest class of utter poverty lies like a gulf before the whole of the working classes, who in spite of all averages live a precarious life; the failure in the game of life which entails on a rich man an unambitious retirement, and on a well-to-do man a life of dependence and laborious shifts, drags a working man down into that hell of irredeemable degradation.[3]

Morris, whatever else he may have been, was a sound student of history,—not of its battles and its dates, but of its meaning, its significance.   He saw its continuity, and so seeing, he held the world in his hands.   He had the organic conception of society, which is to say that he understood life.   In addition, he had a passion for its wholeness, and he believed in the unity of man's powers. He did not profess to be a metaphysician, and it is doubtful whether he would have labelled himself even a thinker.   He formulated no system by which every riddle of the universe was solvable.   His theory of the social order does not, it is true, grasp all of the facts, nor does he always see the bearing of isolated facts; yet he never failed to see the center.   And because of what he lived and thought and spoke, he is nevertheless one of the world's courageous thinkers and doers.   The so-

[3]Morris, *Architecture*, etc., p. 185-190.

called practical man may fling at him the epithet "Idealist!" Yes, but he did not shut himself and his ideals up in a splendid Palace of Art. Persistently and nobly he strove for the happiness of all those to whom our industrial order forbids happiness; persistently and nobly he strove for a reorganization of society based on the fundamental need of man for intelligent work. Give man intelligent work, is Morris's answer to the social question of how to obtain a whole and worthy life. That he dreamed dreams and saw visions is not denied. So also have all noble souls whose work has resulted in progress for mankind. "Visions are the creators and feeders of the world," said George Eliot. "Faith and Utopias are the noblest exercise of the human reason," said William James. "It is the duty," corroborated Max Mueller, "of scholars and philosophers not to shrink from holding and expressing quixotic opinions; for, if I read the history of the world rightly, the victory of reason over unreason, and the whole progress of our race, have generally been achieved by such fools as ourselves, 'rushing in where angels fear to tread,' till after a time, the track becomes beaten, and even angels are no longer afraid."

BIBLIOGRAPHY

ARNOLD, MATTHEW: *Culture and Anarchy.* London, 1875.
Arts and Crafts Essays: By members of the Arts and Crafts Exhibition Society. With a Preface by William Morris. London, 1893.
BAX, E. BELFORT, VICTOR, DAVE, AND MORRIS, WILLIAM: *A Short Account of the Commune of Paris.* London, 1886.
BOOTH, CHARLES: *Labor and Life of the People.* London, 1891.
BOOTH, CHARLES: *Pauperism.* London, 1892.
BOOTH, GENERAL WILLIAM: *In Darkest England and the Way Out.* London and New York, 1891.
Bulletin, United States Bureau of Labor, No. 70
CARLYLE, THOMAS: *Miscellaneous Essays.* London, 1899.
CARLYLE, THOMAS: *Chartism.* In vol. 4, *Critical and Miscellaneous Essays.* New York, 1899.
CARLYLE, THOMAS: *Past and Present.* New York, 1913.
CARVER, T. N.: "Machinery and the Laborer," in *Quarterly Journal of Economics,* Vol. 22:210 ff.
CARY, ELIZABETH LUTHER: *William Morris, Poet, Craftsman, Socialist.* New York and London, 1902.
CHEYNEY, E. P.: *Introduction to Social and Industrial History of England.* New York, 1905.
CLARK, J. B.: *The Philosophy of Wealth.* Boston, 1896.
CLARKE, WILLIAM: "William Morris," in *New England Magazine,* 3:740 ff.
Commonweal, The: The Official Journal of the Socialist League. 6 volumes. Nos. 1-253. From February, 1885 to December, 1890.
COLLINGWOOD, W. G.: *The Life and Work of Ruskin.* Boston, 1893.
CRANE, WALTER: "William Morris", *Scribner's Magazine,* 22:88ff.
DAY, LEWIS FORMAN: *William Morris and His Art. The Art Manual.* London, 1899.
DENTON, WILLIAM: *England in the Fifteenth Century.* London, 1888.
DICKENSON, THOMAS HERBERT: "William Morris and Aesthetic Socialism," in *Arena,* 36:613-7.
DYER, HENRY: *Evolution of Industry.* New York, 1895.
ELY, RICHARD T.: *Socialism and Social Reform.* New York, 1894.
Fabian Essays in Socialism. Edited by G. Bernard Shaw. London, 1899.
FAY, C. R.: *Co-operation at Home and Abroad.* London, 1908.
FYFFE, C. A.: *A History of Modern Europe.* New York, 1896.
GIBBINS, H. DEB.: *Industry in England.* New York, 1906.
GRAHAM, WILLIAM: *The Social Problem.* London, 1886.
GUTHRIE, W. B.: *Socialism Before the French Revolution.* New York, 1907.

GUYOT, Y.: *Sophismes Socialistes et Faits Economiques.* Paris, 1908.

HARRISON, FREDERIC: *Early Victorian Literature.* London, 1895.

HEWLETT, MAURICE: "William Morris," in *National Review,* 17:818 ff.

HOBSON, J. A.: *John Ruskin, Social Reformer.* Boston, 1898.

HOBSON, J. A.: *Problems of Poverty.* London, 1891.

HOBSON, J. A.: *The Problem of the Unemployed.* London, 1896.

HOBSON, J. A.: *The Social Problem.* New York, 1902.

HYNDMAN, H. M.: *The Record of an Adventurous Life.* New York, 1911.

HYNDMAN, H. M., AND MORRIS, WILLIAM: *A Summary of the Principles of Socialism.* London, 1884.

HUBBARD, ELBERT: *A William Morris Book.* East Aurora, New York, 1907.

HUTCHINS, B. L.: *The Public Health Agitation, 1833-1848.*

HUTCHINSON, B. L., AND HARRISON, A.: *A History of Factory Legislation.* London, 1910.

Industrial Education. Published by The American Federation of Labor, March, 1910.

JAMES, WILLIAM: *Talks to Teachers on Psychology and to Students on Some of Life's Ideals.* New York, 1906.

LEE, FRANCIS WATTS: ed. *William Morris, Poet, Artist, Socialist.* A Selection from his Writings together with a Sketch of the Man. New York, 1891.

LOEB, JACQUES: *Comparative Physiology of the Brain and Comparative Psychology.* New York, 1903.

KIRKUP, THOMAS: *A History of Socialism.* London, 1909.

MACKAIL, J. W.: "The Genius of William Morris," in *Independent Review,* 11:51-57.

MACKAIL, J. W.: *The Life of William Morris.* 2 volumes. New York and London, 1901.

MACKAIL, J. W.: *William Morris.* London, 1901.

MACKAIL, J. W.: *William Morris and his Circle.* London, 1907.

MARX, KARL: *Capital.* Translated from the third German edition by Samuel Moore and E. Aveling. London and New York, 1889.

MONTGOMERY, D. H.: *The Leading Facts of English History.* Boston, 1901.

MORLEY, HENRY (Editor): *The Ideal Commonwealth.* New York, 1908.

MORRIS, WILLIAM: *Architecture, Industry and Wealth.* New York, 1902. (Cited as *Architecture,* etc.).

MORRIS, WILLIAM: *Architecture and History of Westminster Abbey.* London, 1902.

MORRIS, WILLIAM: *Art and its Producers and The Arts and Crafts of To-day.* London, 1901.

MORRIS, WILLIAM: *The Defence of Guenevere and Other Poems.* London, 1889.

MORRIS, WILLIAM: *A Dream of John Ball.* London, 1895.

MORRIS, WILLIAM: *The Earthly Paradise.* 3 vols. Boston, 1878.
MORRIS, WILLIAM: *Hopes and Fears for Art.* London and New York, 1905.
MORRIS, WILLIAM: *How I Became a Socialist.* London, n.d.
MORRIS, WILLIAM: *A King's Lesson.* London, 1901.
MORRIS, WILLIAM: *Letters on Socialism.* Partly reprinted in *Poet-Lore,* 7:473 ff., and 543 ff. London, 1884.
MORRIS, WILLIAM: *The Life and Death of Jason.* London, 1889.
MORRIS, WILLIAM: *Love is Enough, or the Freeing of Pharamond.* London, 1889.
MORRIS, WILLIAM, AND BAX, E. BELFORT: *The Manifesto of the Socialist League.* London, 1885.
MORRIS, WILLIAM: *Monopoly; or, How Labor is Robbed.* London, 1890.
MORRIS, WILLIAM: *News From Nowhere, or An Epoch of Rest.* Boston, 1891, also London, 1912.
MORRIS, WILLIAM: *Poems by the Way.* London and New York, 1900.
MORRIS, WILLIAM: *The Reward of Labor: a Dialogue*: London. n.d.
MORRIS, WILLIAM: *Signs of Change.* London, 1888.
MORRIS, WILLIAM AND BAX, E. BELFORT: *Socialism, Its Growth and Outcome.* London, 1893.
MORRIS, WILLIAM: *The Story of Sigurd the Volsung.* London, 1893.
MORRIS, WILLIAM: *The Tables Turned; or, Nupkins Awakened.* London, 1887.
MORRIS, WILLIAM: *A Tale of the House of the Wolfings.* London, 1889.
MORRIS, WILLIAM: *True and False Society.* London, 1888.
MORRIS, WILLIAM: *Under an Elm-Tree, or, Thoughts in the Country-Side.* London, 1891.
MORRIS, WILLIAM: *The Collected Works of William Morris,* 24 vols. London, 1912.
NOYES, ALFRED: *William Morris.* London, 1908.
PODMORE, FRANK: *Robert Owen.* 2 vols. New York, 1907.
POYNTER, EDWARD J.: *Lectures on Art.* London, 1897.
RAE, JOHN: *Contemporary Socialism.* London, 1901.
ROYCE, JOSIAH: *The Religious Aspect of Philosophy.* Boston, 1891.
RUSKIN, JOHN: *Fors Clavigera.* 3 vols. London, 1907.
RUSKIN, JOHN: *Modern Painters.* 5 vols. Boston, 1913.
RUSKIN, JOHN: *Munera Pulveris.* New York, 1891.
RUSKIN, JOHN: *On the Old Road.* Sunnyside, 1885.
RUSKIN, JOHN: *The Political Economy of Art.* New York, 1912.
RUSKIN, JOHN: *Praeterita.* New York, 1886.
RUSKIN, JOHN: *The Stones of Venice.* 3 vols. Boston, 1913.
RUSKIN, JOHN: *Unto This Last.* New York, 1901.
SCHAEFFLE, A.: *The Quintessence of Socialism.* London, 1892.
SCHMOLLER, G.: *Grundfragen der Socialpolitik und der Volkswirtschaftslehre.* Leipzig, 1904.

SCOTT, TEMPLE: *A Bibliography of the Works of William Morris.* London, 1895.

SMITH, J. ALLEN: *The Spirit of American Government.* New York, 1902.

SPARGO, JOHN: *Socialism.* New York, 1906.

SPARGO, JOHN: "Women and the Socialist Movement," in *International Socialist Review,* 8:449-55.

STICKLEY, GUSTAV: *Catalogue of Craftsman Furniture.* New York, 1909.

TRAILL, H. D., AND MANN, J. S.: *Social England.* Volume 6. New York and London, 1904.

TRIGGS, O. L.: "The Socialist Thread in the Life and Work of William Morris," in *Poet-Lore,* 5:113 ff., and 5:210 ff.

VALLANCE, AYMER: *William Morris, His Art, His Writings, and His Public Life.* London, 1898.

VASARI, GIORGIO: *The Lives of the Most Eminent Painters, Sculptors, and Architects.* London, 1850-52; also London, 1912.

VEBLEN, THORSTEN B.: *The Theory of the Leisure Class.* New York, 1899.

WALLACE, ALFRED RUSSELL: *Social Environment and Moral Progress.* New York, 1913.

WEBB, SIDNEY AND BEATRICE: *The History of Trade Unionism.* London and New York, 1894.

WEBB, SIDNEY AND BEATRICE: *Industrial Democracy.* London and New York, 1902.

WEBB, SIDNEY: *Socialism in England.* London, 1890.

INDEX